Your New Life in Christ

A Twelve-week Self-study on Basic Bible Doctrines

Michael H. Clarensau

Gospel Publishing House
Springfield, Missouri
02–0766

Unless otherwise indicated, all Scripture quotations are taken from the HOLY BIBLE: NEW INTERNATIONAL VERSION. Copyright ©1973, 1978, 1984 by International Bible Society. Used by permission of Zondervan Publishing House.

3rd Printing 1998

©1991 by Gospel Publishing House, Springfield, Missouri 65802-1894. All rights reserved. No part of this book may be reproduced, stored in a retrieval system, or transmitted in any form or by any means—electronic, mechanical, photocopy, recording, or otherwise—without prior written permission of the copyright owner, except brief quotations used in connection with reviews in magazines or newspapers.

Library of Congress Catalog Card Number 90-83497
International Standard Book Number 0-88243-766-6
Printed in the United States of America

Table of Contents

How To Use This Book   5

Week One: Christ in You   7
    Day One: What Has Happened to Me?   7
    Day Two: What about My Past?   8
    Day Three: Now and Forever   10
    Day Four: How Can I Know It's Real?   11
    Day Five: A New-found Desire   12

Week Two: But Who Is Jesus?   16
    Day One: Where Jesus Came From   16
    Day Two: How Jesus Came   17
    Day Three: How Jesus Lived   18
    Day Four: Why Jesus Died   19
    Day Five: Jesus' Return   20

Week Three: Our God and Father   24
    Day One: God Is Holy   24
    Day Two: God Is Love   26
    Day Three: God Has All Power   27
    Day Four: God Is Three in One   29
    Day Five: God Is Sovereign   30

Week Four: The Bible, The Basis of Our Belief   34
    Day One: The Bible—God's Word   34
    Day Two: The Authority of the Bible   35
    Day Three: The Bible—A Map for Living   37
    Day Four: Making Scripture a Matter of the Heart   38
    Day Five: Regular Bible Study   39

Week Five: Prayer, Praise, and Worship   43
    Day One: The How and Why of Prayer   43
    Day Two: Why Praise?   45
    Day Three: Devotion—An Attitude of Life   46
    Day Four: Man Proposes, God Disposes   48
    Day Five: Corporate Praise   49

Week Six: The Kind of Conflict We're In   53
    Day One: Cosmic Warfare   53
    Day Two: Know the Enemy   54
    Day Three: Know Where the Battle Is   55
    Day Four: Know Your Commander in Chief   57
    Day Five: Know the End   58

Week Seven: Living Life by the Spirit   61
    Day One: Jesus' Promise of the Holy Spirit   61
    Day Two: The Holy Spirit—God's Spirit   62
    Day Three: The Day of Pentecost   64
    Day Four: Power for Witnessing   65
    Day Five: Power for Daily Living   66

Week Eight: A Life of Love by Grace through Faith   70
    Day One: Grace   70
    Day Two: What Is Faith?   71
    Day Three: An Outpouring of Love   72
    Day Four: Love in Practice   74
    Day Five: Putting It All Together   75

Week Nine: Becoming Like Jesus   78
    Day One: Following the Master   78
    Day Two: Called to Servanthood   79
    Day Three: Obedience, the Key   81
    Day Four: The Fruit of the Spirit   82
    Day Five: Transformed by His Power   83

Week Ten: The People of God   87
    Day One: What Is the Church?   87
    Day Two: The Head of the Church   89
    Day Three: "Body-building"   90
    Day Four: A Call to Ministry   91
    Day Five: In Fellowship   93

Week Eleven: The Church in Action—I   96
    Day One: Discipling/Teaching   96
    Day Two: Water Baptism   98
    Day Three: Holy Communion   99
    Day Four: Praying for the Sick   100
    Day Five: What Is My Part?   101

Week Twelve: The Church in Action—II   104
    Day One: The Ministry of Reconciliation   104
    Day Two: A Heart of Love   105
    Day Three: Sharing the Faith   107
    Day Four: Discipling—The Next Step   108
    Day Five: Reaching the World   109

How To Use This Book

Your New Life in Christ is a program of discipleship designed specifically for the new Christian. Its aims are

- to teach the fundamental principles of the Christian life,
- to introduce God's Word as the Christian's source of faith and conduct,
- to explain that prayer is communion with God, and
- to promote a daily time of devotion and communion with God.

Perhaps you have been introduced to a brother or sister in Christ who will help you with this study. Your pastor can also be of great assistance as you learn more about the Christian life. Take advantage of the help God has provided for you in the lives of these special friends.

On the other hand, if you are doing this study on your own, call on the Holy Spirit to guide you (see John 16:13). Each day a special time of Bible study has been outlined for you. These devotional times are important because through them you will learn the truths of God and receive guidance for living this new life He has given you.

Each day you will be reading several verses from the Bible. In order to locate them, you may need to refer to the table of contents page in the front of your Bible. There you will find that the Bible is actually many books and they make up two "testaments" (which means "promise"), the Old Testament and the New Testament.

To locate, for example, John 3:16, you start by locating the Book of John. You will see four books that are called John in the New Testament. They are John (or St. John in the King James Version), 1 John, 2 John, and 3 John. Since there is no number in front of "John" in John 3:16, this verse is in the Book of John. After turning to the page indicated by the table of contents, you will find that the Book of John, and all other books of the Bible, is divided into chapters and verses. The digit "3" in John 3:16 indicates the chapter and "16" indicates the verse. Therefore, by locating chapter 3 and then the 16th verse within that chapter, you will have arrived at John 3:16.

Finding Bible verses becomes quite easy with practice, once you know the general location of the books, and soon you'll find little need for the table of contents page.

You will need a pen or pencil for responding to some parts of these studies. For example, you may be asked to complete a verse of Scripture by filling in the blanks.

At the close of each day's study you will notice a time of prayer is encouraged. Prayer is our communication with God. If you are not sure how to pray, simply begin to talk to God. Prayer requires no special words or phrases; the Bible shows that prayer is a believer's conversation with God. Of course, because God is who we are talking to, we certainly do not want to be flippant or disrespectful in how we pray, but we need not allow that to intimidate us either. Just express yourself and your thoughts to God. Some of the Bible studies in this book suggest a prayer topic. Use such suggestions as guidelines but don't be limited by them. You are now God's child, and He wants you to enter into communication with Him through prayer.

You will notice five Bible studies for each week of this twelve-week program. The New International Version has been used throughout because of its suitability for both private reading and public worship. Day six is your opportunity to search other verses of the Bible for yourself. This part of the program will help you begin to develop your own devotional time.

Day seven closes each week with an outline that will take you through a review of and reflection on what you have learned through the week. Reflection is a critical part of growing as a Christian; it helps solidify what the Lord is doing in your life.

You will also notice that two Bible passages are to be memorized each week. They are important to the truths you will be learning, and such memorization will also get you started in an important practice: committing God's Word to memory.

If you are doing this study with the help of someone, plan to meet each week so that he or she can help answer questions you may have. This weekly time is very important and should not be bypassed. As you meet with your Christian friend, besides asking questions, ask for help with any struggles of your new life.

Don't rush through this book. Spiritual growth doesn't come overnight. Do each lesson carefully.

Welcome to your new life in Christ.

Week One: Christ in You

BIBLE VERSES TO MEMORIZE:

2 Corinthians 5:17—"If anyone is in Christ, he is a new creation: the old has gone, the new has come!"

Romans 8:1–2—"There is now no condemnation for those who are in Christ Jesus, because through Christ Jesus the law of the Spirit of life set me free from the law of sin and death."

Week One: Christ in You

Day One: What Has Happened to Me?

Key Verses: John 3:16; Ephesians 2:1–10

How exciting it is to be a Christian! Imagine God Almighty loving you enough to enter into history and draw you to himself. Nothing in this world can compare with what Jesus Christ has done in your life.

A Gift for All

▶ Read John 3:16

John 3:16 is perhaps the most familiar verse in the Bible; it shares a very special truth. "God so loved the world that he gave his one and only Son that whoever believes in him

_____ _____ _____ _____

_____ _____ _____."

What an incredible truth! You will live forever because you have believed that Jesus Christ is God's son and He came to die for you. Now even the pains of death that will someday take life from your physical body cannot touch the eternal life that God has given you. Take time right now to thank Him for that special gift.

Changing—His Way

▶ Read Ephesians 2:1–10

Besides bringing you eternal life, Jesus Christ has come to change your present life. He wants to change you for the better; He wants you to be like Him.

In the New Testament, a man named Paul of Tarsus underwent just such a change. He wrote a letter to the believers at Ephesus. Notice in verse three that he includes himself as one who once lived to please himself. (For a fuller picture of Paul's conversion, you may wish to read Acts 9.)

Jesus has come into your life to make you more like Him and to place within you the desires and motives to live by the Spirit. Can you sense some of the changes His presence in your heart has already begun to make? Take a few minutes and list them.

_____

_____

In the coming weeks we will be talking more and more about what Jesus wants to do in your life. Now enjoy the privilege of prayer and thank God again for the gift He has given you and the love He has shown you; then express your desire to be what He wants you to be. Ask Him to show you the changes He wants to make in your life.

Week One: Christ in You

Day Two: What about My Past?

Key Verses: Psalm 103:12; Romans 1:7; 1 Corinthians 1:2; 2 Corinthians 5:17; Colossians 2:13

Perhaps your most troubling concern as a new member of God's family is your past. The Bible identifies the enemy of the believer as Satan, which means "adversary," or the devil, which means "slanderer." So don't be surprised that you are tempted to be discouraged and ashamed about the sins of your past. But remember that Jesus, our Savior, is more than a match for the devil. And He's already taken care of your past.

A Brand New Life

▶ Read 2 Corinthians 5:17

What did verse 17 call you? That's right. A new creation. "The old has _____, the _____ has come!" Did you read that carefully? So that you might be informed about our common enemy, we will talk about Satan more in the coming weeks. Right now, however, memorize this verse; it's ammunition against him.

A Saint

▶ Read Romans 1:7; 1 Corinthians 1:2

Forget the definition of the word "saint" in some parts of the religious world and the world at large. Learn the New Testament definition: *all* believers in Christ, from the child to the deathbed penitent. The term is not reserved for believers who achieve some kind of spiritual seniority.

"Saint" means one God has called to serve Him, a Christian. That's you. So when you hear references to "the saints" or read about "saints" in the Bible, consider yourself among that number.

Alive through Forgiveness

▶ Read Colossians 2:13

You were spiritually dead in your sins, but your Lord has made you alive by _____ all your sins. No matter what kind of life you lived before you gave yourself to Jesus, you have been forgiven.

Forgiven Completely

▶ Read Psalm 103:12

Many people who have been Christians for years continue to struggle with sins of their past. They live lives of guilt even though God has forgiven them, even though He has taken away every reason for that guilt. This verse says that our sin is removed as far as the _____ _____ _____ _____ _____.

Now take time to pray, and thank God for His forgiveness. Then ask Him to help you forget what He has forgiven.

Week One: Christ in You

Day Three: Now and Forever

Key Verses: Matthew 28:20; John 14:2; Romans 8:1–2; Colossians 3:4

Perhaps the most exciting aspect of the Christian life is that Jesus Christ has done more than just remove and forgive the past. He has taken care of your future, and He walks with you today. Your study today focuses on what that means.

No More Condemnation

▶ Read Romans 8:1–2

Because you have given your life to Jesus, there is no condemnation from God in your future. You have been given a new start, and you face a future of blessings. The second verse continues by saying that this freedom from condemnation comes "because through Christ Jesus the law of the _____ _____ _____ set me _____ from the law of _____ _____ _____." That's what this course is all about: learning what it means to live according to the "Spirit of life."

An Ever-present Friend

▶ Read Matthew 28:20

"I am with you _____." For the rest of your life do not forget those words. Although the Christian life is not free of troubles, Jesus promises that He will always be with you. As you grow in your new life, learn to call on Christ for strength for every situation.

Why don't you stop right now and talk to God about the problems you are facing? Ask Him for encouragement; ask Him for wisdom to know what to do and courage to do it. He's with you all the way.

A Forever Home

▶ Read John 14:2; Colossians 3:4

These exciting verses deal with our more distant future as God's children. In His last hours upon this earth, Jesus gave the promise that He was going "to _____ _____ _____ for you." That place is heaven, and its beauty will be beyond anything we could ever imagine.

Jesus Christ made his first appearance as an ordinary carpenter. Colossians 3:4 speaks of a day when He will appear in all His glory and majesty—and we will be there with Him. For all eternity we shall live in His glory. What a fantastic future!

Now as you pray, express your love for Him and thank Him for all that He has prepared for you. Thank Him for always being with you. Begin today to talk with Him about your struggles in life.

Week One: Christ in You

Day Four: How Can I Know It's Real?

Key Verses: John 6:37; 7:17; Romans 8:38–39; 1 Corinthians 1:8–9; 2 Timothy 1:12

The Christian life is begun by faith and lived by faith. Faith means believing strongly enough to stake one's life (or action) on what is believed. One of the themes of the Gospel of John is believing that Jesus is who He said He is (see John 20:31). If you believe in a person, you believe the things that person says. Christian faith is about believing what God has said in His Word, the Bible, and acting on it. Let's look at some Bible verses that will help clarify this matter of faith.

Knowing Whom You Believe

▶ Read 2 Timothy 1:12

The apostle Paul wrote, "I _____ whom I have _____." Paul was convinced that his faith was not misplaced: Jesus was the Messiah, the one the Old Testament had said was coming, and He was absolutely trustworthy. The more you get to know Jesus through studying the Bible (especially the Gospels), talking about Him, and learning to pray—the stronger your faith will grow in Him. Learn all you can about Jesus.

Knowing through Experience

▶ Read John 7:17

Jesus told those who doubted Him to test His teaching simply by doing it, by choosing to "do God's will." By confessing your sin and asking God's forgiveness, you have begun doing God's will (see 2 Peter 3:9). Jesus Christ has come into your life and forgiven you of your sin and given you eternal life. Jesus said He will lighten peoples' loads if they come to Him (see Matthew 11:28–30). Hasn't that been your experience?

The enemy will try to make you doubt what you have experienced by believing Jesus. Stand with Paul and proclaim, "I know whom I have believed."

He Has Received You

▶ Read John 6:37; Romans 8:38–39

You have come to Him and asked Him to take control of your life, and He has promised that He will not turn away anyone who approaches Him in faith. Thank God for lovingly welcoming anyone as His child when that person comes to Him.

Once we have come to Him and He has received us, Romans 8:38–39 tells us that *nothing* shall separate us from the love of God that is in Christ Jesus. That's a promise. When we come to Him, nothing can separate us from Him. We are His as long as we continue to give ourselves to Him.

He Keeps His Word

▶ Read 1 Corinthians 1:8–9

One thing you will learn in your relationship with God is that He is faithful. He never fails. These verses proclaim His faithfulness to you as someone He has called. And furthermore, it tells us that every promise that God has made is trustworthy.

Now offer prayer to God. Thank Him that He never fails. Thank Him that you can always depend on Him. Ask Him to help you overcome doubt. Ask Him to help you speak boldly the words of 2 Timothy 1:12: "I know whom I have believed."

Week One: Christ in You

Day Five: A New-found Desire

Key Verses: Hebrews 10:19–22; James 4:8; Revelation 3:20

When a person's spirit comes to life in God, his desire for God, his Creator, is awakened; he wants to know God intimately. The Psalmist wrote, "As the deer pants for streams of water, so my soul pants for you, O God" (Psalm 42:1). Don't ignore that desire; follow it. It will nourish your spiritual life.

An Invitation to Fellowship

▶ Read Revelation 3:20

The Laodicean church thought they had it all (see verse 17). Jesus told them it was just the opposite: They were poverty-stricken. But then He said, in so many words, invite Me into the situation; I will right it. If He wanted fellowship with the spiritually blind and self-righteous, think how much more He wants to fellowship with those who are seeking Him—you!

Let Us Respond

▶ Read Hebrews 10:19–22

What are these verses encouraging you to do?

_____

_____

The desire to be close to God can be lost. Jesus identified some of the ways that can happen: persecution, worries of this life, the deceitfulness of wealth (see Matthew 13:18–22). Ask God to guard you against those things and help you understand His Word.

Getting Closer

▶ Read James 4:8

We are told that as we draw close to God, He will in turn draw close to us. But how do we draw close to Him? By cleansing and purifying our lives (see Psalm 24:3–4). We must be working toward being the Christian that He wants us to be.

Write James 4:8 and begin now to let its words speak to you.

_____

_____

Now talk to Him and express your desire to know Him more fully. Then ask for His guidance as you try to become all that He has planned for you.

Week One: Christ in You

Day Six

Verses of the Bible I read:

What did they teach me?

What questions do I have?

What do I need to talk to God about?

Week One: Christ in You

Day Seven

What has God shown me through His Word this week?

What questions do I have?

What changes have I seen in my life this week?

If someone asked me to describe the change in my life, I would tell them . . .

Week Two: But Who Is Jesus?

BIBLE VERSES TO MEMORIZE:

Isaiah 53:5—"He was pierced for our transgressions, he was crushed for our iniquities; the punishment that brought us peace was upon him, and by his wounds we are healed."

Colossians 1:19—"God was pleased to have all his fullness dwell in him [i.e., Jesus]."

Week Two: But Who Is Jesus?

Day One: Where Jesus Came From

Key Verses: Micah 5:2; John 8:58–59; 17:5; Revelation 1:8; 22:13

Last week's material focused on the Christ-centered life. This week focuses on Jesus Christ himself. We worship Jesus Christ as Savior and Lord because He is the Son of God. Let's see what the Bible has to say about Him.

From One of the Smallest Towns

▶Read Micah 5:2

This verse foretold the birth of Christ many hundreds of years before that first Christmas in Bethlehem. Despite Bethlehem's insignificance among the villages and towns of Israel, God picked it for the birthplace of His Son, our Savior.

But notice that this verse points out that the Savior had origins "from ancient times." Only His human life began at Bethlehem.

From before the Beginning

▶Read John 8:58–59; Revelation 1:8; 22:13

These verses show us that Jesus has no beginning. He is as eternal as God. (The Jews understood what Jesus was claiming; that's why they were ready to stone Him.)

Write Revelation 22:13 here:

_____

_____

Note that Jesus identified himself the same way God did in 1:8.

From a Place of Honor

▶Read John 17:5

John 17 is a prayer that Jesus prayed toward the end of His earthly life. In this verse, His prayer is that He might return to the place of honor He had before coming to Earth. (The material in day two will illustrate that this prayer was answered.)

As we study the Bible, we often encounter truths beyond our understanding. This is one: Jesus had no beginning. Furthermore, He left a place of honor on our behalf; He loved us that much. For that we ought to praise and worship Him every day. Why not make that a part of your prayer time today?

Week Two: But Who Is Jesus?

Day Two: How Jesus Came

Key Verses: Luke 1:35; Acts 7:54–56; Colossians 1:15–20; Daniel 7:13–14

The greatest story ever told began one ordinary night in the ordinary village of Bethlehem: The Son of God was born and salvation was brought to humanity. (You can read about it in detail in Matthew 1 and 2 or Luke 1 and 2.)

As the Son of God

▶Read Colossians 1:15–20

As fantastic as it may seem, the helpless infant in the manger was the Son of God, "for God was pleased to have all his fullness dwell in him" (v. 19). One of the greatest expressions of Christ's love for us is that He left His position of honor in heaven and came to be a servant of and sacrifice for mankind. This coming of God as a human into history is called the Incarnation.

As the Son of Man

▶Read Acts 7:54–56; Daniel 7:13–14

Besides being fully God, Jesus was also thoroughly human. Daniel, in one of his visions, was the first to refer to the Messiah as "son of man." Jesus used it often of himself, more than eighty times in the Gospels. Stephen, the first person to be executed for following Jesus, had a vision like Daniel's. He saw Jesus, the Son of Man, exalted to God's right hand. Here again the Jews knew what was meant by the expression—The person they knew as Jesus of Nazareth was being equated with God.

Conceived by the Holy Spirit

▶Read Luke 1:35

Luke tells us something special about Jesus' entrance into humanity: He was conceived by the power of the Holy Spirit. God worked a miracle in the body of Mary so that she would give birth to this special child. This is what is known as the virgin birth of Christ, for He had no earthly father. Mary was so overwhelmed by the experience that she burst out in praise (see Luke 1:46–55).

Week Two: But Who Is Jesus?

Day Three: How Jesus Lived

Key Verses: John 19:4; Hebrews 4:15; 5:8–9; 1 Peter 2:22

Learning about Jesus can take a lifetime. But this is the truth about Jesus that makes our salvation possible: He was perfect. He lived a life free of sin. Almost daily we come face to face with our imperfections, but Jesus led a sinless life. Let's read what the Bible has to say about Him.

A Sinless Life

▶Read John 19:4; 1 Peter 2:22

Here we find two witnesses to the spotless life of Jesus: the apostle Peter and Pontius Pilate. What great diversity in sources! Peter lived daily with Jesus, watching every move His Master made so that he might be like Him. If Jesus had fallen short in any area, Peter would have known.

Pilate, on the other hand, met Jesus in court. He sought to find out why accusations were being brought against Jesus. Though the easiest avenue for his administration would have been to hurry the proceedings along, even Pilate had to admit that he could find no fault in Jesus.

A Worthy Sacrifice

▶Read Hebrews 4:15; 5:8–9

These verses give us the two reasons why Jesus' sinless life is so important. Can you find those reasons?

1. _____

2. _____

First of all, because Jesus was sinless, He alone is worthy to be the sacrifice for our sins. In the Old Testament, God had instructed His followers to sacrifice certain animals to cover their sins. These animals had to be perfect, without blemish, to be acceptable as sacrifices. In the same way, Jesus too had to be perfect if He was to be the sacrifice for the sin of mankind.

Second, Hebrews tells us that Jesus experienced the same temptations and testing that you and I do, and He did so without sinning. Nevertheless, He has an understanding of our struggles and has become an example of how to handle them.

Week Two: But Who Is Jesus?

Day Four: Why Jesus Died

Key Verses: Isaiah 53:5; 1 Corinthians 15:20–22; 2 Timothy 1:10; 1 Peter 2:24

You probably already know a great deal about Jesus' death on the Cross and His return to life. Even so, let's look at a few important verses that teach some special truths about the sacrifice of Jesus.

To Take Our Suffering

▶Read Isaiah 53:5; 1 Peter 2:24

As you combine the thoughts of these verses in your mind,

what understanding of Jesus' sacrifice do you see? What does His death mean for you?

___

Jesus took our place in the punishment of death so that we could have eternal life. Take a few moments to thank Him for His love.

To Be Victorious over Death

▶Read 1 Corinthians 15:20–22; 2 Timothy 1:10

Adam began it; Jesus finished it. That is, death came into the human race by Adam's disobedience in the Garden of Eden, and life came through Jesus Christ's obedience in the Garden of Gethsemane ("Not my will, but yours be done"—Luke 22:42).

Because Jesus came back from the dead, Paul says we can expect the same thing when we die. Though our physical bodies may one day return to the dust, we can know that we will rise on that day when God brings His Kingdom to fulfillment. What a wonderful promise!

Today spend time loving God in prayer. Thank Him that He cared about and loved you enough to die on the Cross. And thank Him that He conquered death by coming back to life.

Week Two: But Who Is Jesus?

Day Five: Jesus' Return

Key Verses: John 14:3; Acts 1:11; 1 Thessalonians 5:2; Titus 2:13

Your salvation is sure. Nothing can undo what Jesus has done on your behalf—that's fact, that's history. And you are blessed because you have believed without being an eyewitness of those events (see John 20:29). But a day is coming when you will see for yourself whom you have believed, and believed in. Jesus Christ is going to return to take us to be with Him forever.

It Is Certain

▶Read John 14:3; Acts 1:11

Jesus himself told His disciples that He would return. After all, He was going away specifically to prepare a special place for each of them (and each of us). And then later the angels reminded and reassured them of Jesus' return: He would come back in the same way they saw Him go into heaven. One day all believers will have the glorious blessing of being received by Jesus and shown to that residence custom-built by Him. That's a promise.

It Is the Blessed Hope

▶Read Titus 2:13

Write out Titus 2:13.

_____

_____

In encouraging his young friend and fellow worker Titus, Paul described the return of Jesus Christ as "the blessed hope."

However, our word "hope" is a little too weak for the Greek word it translates, for it is a certainty, a definite time that is coming. So we put our confidence and trust in the One who has given the promise. Perhaps "the blessed *expectation*" would be closer to the Greek.

He is coming back. How wonderful to know that we will be in the presence of our Lord Jesus! And we will be reunited with any friends who may have died in the faith. There we will rejoice with our brothers and sisters in Him for all eternity.

It Will be Sudden

▶Read 1 Thessalonians 5:2

One of the things the Bible teaches about Jesus' return is its suddenness. Jesus himself compared it to lightning (see Luke 17:24). The apostle Paul, writing to believers at Thessalonica, likened it to the nighttime coming of a thief—no warning, no announcement. It will be unexpected and unwanted by those who don't know Jesus as Savior.

But it will be joyously welcomed by those like you who know He is coming and are looking forward to His return. Why should we be surprised when Jesus comes back? He has told us that He is coming; the angels have proclaimed it as well. No, Christ's return will be no surprise for believers. As a matter of fact, it will be the most joyous occasion we have ever known. For we will celebrate the return of our Master.

Week Two: But Who Is Jesus?

Day Six

Verses of the Bible I read:

What did they teach me?

What questions do I have?

What do I need to talk to God about?

Week Two: But Who Is Jesus?

Day Seven

What has God shown me through His Word this week?

What questions do I have?

What changes have I seen in my life this week?

If someone asked me who Jesus was and is, I would say . . .

Week Three: Our God and Father

BIBLE VERSES TO MEMORIZE

Isaiah 64:8—"O Lord, you are our Father. We are the clay, you are the potter; we are all the work of your hand."

1 John 3:1—"How great is the love the Father has lavished on us, that we should be called the children of God!"

Week Three: Our God and Father

Day One: God Is Holy

Key Verses: Exodus 15:11; Leviticus 11:45; Isaiah 6:3; Revelation 15:4

Not only have you begun a new life as a Christian, you have also entered into a new relationship with God. He is now your Father. In the sense that He created you, He has always been your Father. But now you have begun a spiritual relationship with Him, for He has made you a new creation.

You have naturally become acquainted with God's Son, for it is through Him that you came to God (see John 14:6). But it is important that you know and understand the greatness and wonder of the Almighty God himself.

A Holy God

▶Read Isaiah 6:3

In Isaiah's vision of God's throneroom, the creatures around the throne cried out "_____, _____, _____." This had to be the most overwhelming moment in Isaiah's life: seeing and realizing the awesomeness of God's holiness. Some other Scripture verses can help us understand what God's holiness means.

None Other Like Him

▶Read Exodus 15:11

What does Moses say about God in the first part of this verse?

_____

God is God and there is no other. One aspect of holiness is being separate, set apart; the Bible teaches us that God is separate from, over and above, His creation. He is "majestic in holiness, awesome in glory, working wonders."

Later this week we will talk about His "working wonders." But it is vital that all God's people realize His greatness and His holiness. We cannot really worship God properly unless we have an understanding of who He is.

Our Response

▶Read Leviticus 11:45; Revelation 15:4

These two verses tell us how we are to respond to God's holiness. Leviticus 11:45 tells us that because God is holy, we are to be _____. That is, if we are to be God's people, we are to be like God. God is sinless, righteous, pure. In fact, He is the definition of righteousness. Because His character is holy, so should ours be; we should lead lives different from those in the world. For that reason, God has provided a way to make us pure through the life of His Son, Jesus Christ (see Titus 2:11–12).

Revelation 15:4 tells us that fear and worship are proper responses to God. The fear is not fright so much as respect and honor and adoration. Once we understand who God is, we realize what a privilege we have to acknowledge Him in a relationship with us.

In fact, that's a good place to start your prayer time today. Just spend time thanking Him for His forgiveness, and ask Him to help you recognize His holiness.

Week Three: Our God and Father

Day Two: God Is Love

Key Verses: Psalm 8:3–4; Jeremiah 31:3; John 3:16; Romans 5:8; 1 John 3:1

Yesterday you learned about God's holiness. The more you understand about God's holiness, the more special His love will become to you. For example, though God is holy and thus separate from us, because He is love, He reaches out to us.

Love of a Creator

▶Read Psalm 8:3–4

The psalmist David was often amazed at God's love. And his observations of nature were sometimes what inspired him to contemplate that love. Try it yourself: On a clear night notice the vast array of stars; then realize that the God who spoke those heavenly wonders into existence cares deeply for every part of your life.

Forever Love

▶Read Jeremiah 31:3

"I have loved you with an _____ love." When God commits himself to a love relationship, He gives a love that will endure for all time. You may question that love during difficult circumstances, but He's loving you then too. His promise is of an *everlasting* love.

Love Shows

▶Read John 3:16; Romans 5:8

God's love is active, not passive. If someone told you, "I love you," but never showed that love, you might question such love. But God has proven His love in extraordinary fashion.

Write Romans 5:8 here.

_____

_____

_____

Because God is holy, He despises sin. But He loves the sinner. Even while mankind was rebelling against Him, God sent His Son, Jesus Christ, to sacrifice himself. This is a kind of love the world rarely—if ever—produces.

John 3:16 is already a familiar verse to you by now. It tells us that God gave His Son so that we might not "_____." This verse tells us what mankind faces without God: to die in sin and be separated from God for eternity. But He loves His creation so much that He has opened the way to "_____ _____ life."

Love of a Father

▶Read 1 John 3:1

And because of that love we are now "_____ of God." And even though unbelievers may not recognize us as God's children, that doesn't change the fact any more than it did when people didn't recognize Jesus as God's Son.

Today spend time in prayer thanking God for His deep love for you. It is not a love that is merited; it is a love that comes because of God's generosity, His grace.

Week Three: Our God and Father

Day Three: God Has All Power

Key Verses: Psalm 139:8; Isaiah 43:13; Matthew 19:26; Hebrews 4:13

God is holy, and He is love. In fact, He is the full definition of holiness and love. But He is more: He is all-powerful, all-knowing, and everywhere present—He is the Almighty.

Unlimited Strength

▶Read Isaiah 43:13

What does the last line of that verse say?

_____

_____

God has no limitations. Human beings do. Perhaps that is one reason we have difficulty comprehending His strength and power.

The Bible is full of the acts of God, many of which we call miracles. Just by simple command He can alter the course of nature, reverse sickness, and undo death. Nothing is beyond His power. Let that knowledge give you great security. This unlimited God knows what you need and why and when you need it. No power or force exists that can hinder Him from providing for His children.

Always Everywhere

▶Read Psalm 139:8

Where is God? _____ The Psalmist tells us that no one can escape His presence. Just as God knows no limitations of power, He knows no boundaries to His being. He is too big to be contained by the universe and yet able, at the same time, to live in our hearts. (See Acts 17:24,28.)

This verse also encourages us to know that God is with us always. No matter where we go, He will walk beside us. That's the beauty of this wonderful quality of God.

Knowing All Things

▶Read Hebrews 4:13

What is hidden from God's sight? "_____" God knows it all! No knowledge or truth is beyond Him. What does that mean to you?

_____

_____

The Possibilities of the Impossible

▶Read Matthew 19:26

Write this verse.

_____

_____

That says it all. No situation that you face will ever be more than God can handle. God is more than equal to the occasion—no matter how challenging, no matter how difficult.

Do you have something you need God to help you with? Then tell Him about it through prayer.

Week Three: Our God and Father

Day Four: God Is Three in One

Key Verses: Matthew 3:16–17; 28:19; John 15:26; 17:20,21; 1 Peter 1:2

Because we are finite, having many limitations, we have difficulty comprehending the infinite, limitless God. But the Psalmist reassures us that God realizes "how we are formed, he remembers that we are dust" (Psalm 103:14). Recognizing the limitations of humans, God has not left it to us to find Him; He is the self-revealing God. He has sought mankind from the beginning, calling to Adam in the Garden of Eden, " 'Where are you?' " (Genesis 3:9). This is recorded in the Bible, the place God has most clearly revealed himself. And one of the things we learn about Him there is that He is a triune God, a trinity.

Message of the Trinity

▶Read Matthew 28:19

In this verse, which is called the Great Commission, Jesus sends His disciples out, telling them to baptize in the name of the Father, Son, and Holy Spirit. God wants himself recognized as existing in three Persons. They are identified as Father, Son, and Holy Spirit.

In the days of the Old Testament, God revealed himself as the Father. He was the leader and sustainer of His people, Israel. Then Jesus came to Earth. He is God the Son. After Jesus returned to His place of glory in heaven, the Holy Spirit came to live in the hearts of God's people.

The Trinity in Salvation

▶Read Matthew 3:16–17; 1 Peter 1:2

Here, in these two verses, we see all three persons of the Trinity. At the time of Jesus' baptism, the Spirit came down from heaven, and the Father spoke:

_____

_____

_____

In Peter's letter, we see that all three persons of the Trinity are at work in our salvation.

Work of the Trinity

▶Read John 15:26

Here we get a glimpse of the relationship within the Trinity. "The Counselor [Holy Spirit]... from the Father... will testify about me [Jesus, the Son]." A major part of the ministry of the Holy Spirit is to testify, or speak about, Jesus. This tells us something of the unity of action and purpose within the Trinity, a point the next verse will emphasize.

Unity in the Trinity

▶Read John 17:20–21

How does Jesus describe His relationship with the Father?

_____

It is a picture of complete unity, which addresses the most difficult part of understanding the Trinity: that we do *not* worship three Gods. The three persons of the Trinity are perfectly united as one God. We can't fully understand how that is possible, but He is God, and that is what He has revealed to us of himself.

Praise God that He loves us enough to make himself known to us!

Week Three: Our God and Father

Day Five: God Is Sovereign

Key Verses: Genesis 3:15; Ezekiel 36:27; Joel 2:28; John 14:3; Isaiah 64:8

Have you ever felt like things were out of control? Though we may feel that way, God never does. The Bible teaches that He is Sovereign and that He has a plan that is at work in this world—which nothing can alter. You remember that we have already established God's great power and that no one can prevent Him from doing what He decides to do. Well, God has a plan that He intends to complete in this world. Let's see just what God has in mind.

Promise of Salvation

▶Read Genesis 3:15

When God created humanity, everything was perfect paradise. But when Adam chose to sin rather than obey God, severe consequences followed: sin, sickness, and death. But mankind's sin did not catch God off guard. God revealed to Eve a great plan that would one day right the wrong that she and Adam had done.

God told Eve her "offspring" would crush the head of Satan. That "offspring" is Jesus Christ. When He died on the Cross and rose from the dead, He crushed Satan and his plans. God's plan from the very first, "before the creation of the world" (1 Peter 1:20), was to send His Son, Jesus Christ, to pay the penalty of death for sin and then to overcome death through His resurrection.

The Fact of His Fatherhood

▶Read Isaiah 64:8

As was already mentioned, God is the Father of everyone in the sense that He created everyone. But He is the Father of His people, Christians, in a special, spiritual sense. As such He is to be acknowledged and worshiped and obeyed.

Promise of the Holy Spirit

▶Read Ezekiel 36:27; Joel 2:28

Write the verse from Joel here.

_____

_____

_____

Through the prophets Joel and Ezekiel, God told the people of Israel that one day He would pour out His Spirit upon all people. In the Old Testament, God's Spirit was given only to prophets to speak as intermediate messengers between the people and God. But the day would come, in the plan of God, when His Spirit would be given to all who desired to receive. That day came after Jesus' death and resurrection, according to Acts 2, where Peter uses Joel's words as a sermon text.

Promise of Eternal Life

▶Read John 14:3

What does this verse tell you?

_____

_____

God's plan didn't end with Jesus' death and resurrection. Besides including sending the Holy Spirit, God's plan includes a special place He has prepared for us. One day Jesus will take us to this glorious place and we will be with God forever.

Today, thank God for His sovereignty, for His eternal plan, and for the love that allowed you to be a part of His plan.

Week Three: Our God and Father

Day Six

Verses of the Bible I read:

What did they teach me?

What questions do I have?

What do I need to talk to God about?

Week Three: Our God and Father

Day Seven

What has God shown me through His Word this week?

What questions do I have?

What changes have I seen in my life this week?

If someone asked me about God, how would I describe Him?

Week Four: The Bible, The Basis of Our Belief

BIBLE VERSES TO MEMORIZE:

2 Timothy 3:16—"All Scripture is God-breathed and is useful for teaching, rebuking, correcting and training in righteousness."

Psalm 119:11—"I have hidden your word in my heart that I might not sin against you."

Week Four: The Bible, The Basis of Our Belief

Day One: The Bible—God's Word

Key Verses: John 1:1,14; 20:31; Romans 15:4; 2 Timothy 3:16; 2 Peter 1:21

When you gave your heart and life to Jesus Christ, you were introduced to a book, the Bible. Do you know why? What makes the Bible so special to Christians? In this week's material, we are going to learn about this exceptional book and discover why it is so important to us.

The Origin of the Bible

▶Read 2 Timothy 3:16; 2 Peter 1:21

These verses tell us of Scripture's orgin. The Bible is not just another book written by man; it was inspired, "God-breathed." God the Holy Spirit was intimately involved in the process. That's what makes the Bible unique—its author is actually God. For although God used people to write His book (around forty in fact), its message comes straight from His heart.

Just how God communicated His words to these men is uncertain. (Compare Luke's explanation of how he wrote his

Gospel, 1:1–4, and John's explanation of how he wrote Revelation, 1:1–2, 10.) Nevertheless, we believe all the books of the Bible were equally inspired.

The Divinity of the Bible

▶Read John 1:1,14

Jesus Christ is known as the Word, the Living Word. He is God's eternal message to the world (see John 12:49), a message of love and forgiveness. This message runs throughout the Bible, God's word. If a person says he believes in and accepts God's Son, he should realize that he is accepting His Word, the Bible, as well. (See John 5:39.)

The Reason for the Bible

▶Read John 20:31; Romans 15:4

The previous verses told us how Scripture came to us; these verses tell us why. Look first at the verse from John. He tells us that what he wrote was written so that the reader "may have _____."

God gave His Word so that mankind might know the way of salvation. In the Bible, we are invited to come to God and have a relationship with Him. It also explains how.

Romans 15:4 gives a further reason God gave His Word: to teach us so that we might be instructed and encouraged as we face the struggles of life.

Take time to thank God for the blessing of having His Word to guide you, give you hope and encouragement, and show you the way to live for Him.

Week Four: The Bible, The Basis of Our Belief

Day Two: The Authority of the Bible

Key Verses: Isaiah 40:8; Jeremiah 23:25–29; Matthew 24:35; Galatians 1:8; Hebrews 4:12

The Bible is authoritative. After all, it's God's Word, revealing His will. Believers have recognized it as their "all-sufficient rule for faith and conduct." Therefore, when you need direction, look to the Bible. When you are uncertain about some teaching or practice, look to the Bible. It is trustworthy; make it your standard.

The Truth of the Word

▶Read Jeremiah 23:25–29

Ever since Satan deceived Eve, false teachers have been in the world with their false teachings. They were around in Jeremiah's day; they are around in our day. And they are often just as subtle as Satan. How do we recognize false teaching? First, we learn the truth, God's Word, and then measure all other teachings against it.

The Power of the Word

▶Read Hebrews 4:12

The Bible is great literature—but it is much more than that. This can be demonstrated by the Bible's effect on people: It alone can salvage and transform lives. No other literature has that power.

The Only Word of Salvation

▶Read Galatians 1:8

As you can see from Paul's teaching here, straying from the teaching of God's Word—particularly the gospel—is very serious. Jesus said he was the true and living way. There is no other. (See John 14:6 and Acts 4:12.)

The Eternal Word

▶Read Isaiah 40:8; Matthew 24:35

What is the truth about the Word contained in these two verses?

_____

What does that mean to you?

_____

Thank God for His Word. Today you have seen that we are to hold God's Word, the Bible, in high regard. Ask God to help you as you study His Word, so that it can be a guide to you as you live to please Him.

Week Four: The Bible, The Basis of Our Belief

Day Three: The Bible—A Map for Living

Key Verses: Psalm 119:9,11,105; Proverbs 29:18; James 1:22; 2:26

When you are traveling to a place you have never been before, two great helps to have along are a guide and a map. In this Christian life, we have both: the Holy Spirit and the Bible. Today let's look closely at the map, the Bible.

Restraint from the Word

▶Read Proverbs 29:18

Where would mankind be without God's Word? This verse gives us a clue. Without the guidance of God's word, humanity would certainly be in a much worse condition than it is, rather like the people of Israel after they had given up waiting for Moses to come down from Mt. Sinai (see Exodus 32:7). By living in the manner that God prescribes, people bring glory to God. That ought to be our highest goal.

For Keeping Pure

▶Read Psalm 119:9

How may we keep ourselves pure?

_____

Can you think of ways that your life has changed since you began to read and study God's Word? List some of them below.

_____

_____

_____

For Avoiding Sin

▶Read Psalm 119:11

This week you should be memorizing this verse. It suggests that memorization helps us avoid sin. In other words, we don't want to use our ignorance as an excuse for either doing what we shouldn't or not doing what we should.

To Gain Direction

▶Read Psalm 119:105.

The metaphor of a light is often used to describe God's Word. The Psalmist does that here, implying that God's Word can be relied on for direction in life.

Doing the Word

▶Read James 1:22; 2:26

Finally, James points out that it is not enough to hear God's message; a person's life must be changed by it. Certainly we thank God for His Word and rejoice in it. But more than that, we follow what it says.

For example, our faith should show in how we live. James makes that point in the last half of chapter 2. The Bible tells us how to let it show. The Bible repeats this theme in many places. Our task is to make sure we pay attention and never try to get around its message.

In your prayer time today express to God your desire to do and be what He wants. Then ask Him to show you the truths in His Word. And don't forget to thank Him for what He has already shown you.

Week Four: The Bible, The Basis of Our Belief

Day Four: Making Scripture a Matter of the Heart

Key Verses: Psalm 1:1–2; John 14:26; Philippians 4:8; 2 Peter 1:3–4

This week's material has been emphasizing God's Word, focusing on making it a part of our lives. The material of the last two days of this week identifies ways to do that. The first is by committing verses to memory—which the Bible encourages us to do. Consider the following reasons for doing such memory work.

So You Might Be Reminded

▶Read John 14:26

Jesus promised His disciples that He would send the Holy Spirit to help them remember what He had taught them. That's every believer's promise. But that means you have to learn

Jesus' teachings first. That is, get them in your memory bank like the disciples did. Then you can be reminded in the time that you need them.

So You Might Meditate

▶Read Psalm 1:1–2; Philippians 4:8

What a person thinks is eventually what that person becomes. The Psalmist knew that; so did Paul. So many subtle, corrupting influences are loose in the world that the Christian must take care in preserving the righteous life God has given him. One way this is done is by thinking on God's Holy Word.

As Anchors for Your Belief

▶Read 2 Peter 1:3–4

Do you know what you believe? Do you know what God has promised you as His follower? (Note Psalm 119:148 in the NIV.) You must if you are to survive and grow. He has provided everything you need—"great and precious promises"—to grow strong, to mature, in Christ. In your memory work you have begun to learn those promises. They can serve as anchors to your faith, holding you steady when the doubts and storms of life hit.

Scripture memorization may be difficult, but the Holy Spirit can help. Today, ask God to help you memorize.

Week Four: The Bible, The Basis of Our Belief

Day Five: Regular Bible Study

Key Verses: Acts 17:11; Ephesians 4:14; 1 Peter 2:2

In addition to memorizing verses of Scripture, you need to regularly study God's Word. As we have noted, it is our map and standard as well as our teacher and encourager. You will find in the verses below some special challenges to make regular Bible study important in your life.

To Know the Truth

▶Read Acts 17:11

Why were the believers in Berea described as being of "more noble character than the Thessalonians"? That is, what two responses did the Bereans have to Paul's preaching the gospel to them?

1. _____

2. _____

Such an approach is necessary for determining God's truth.

To Become Stable

▶Read Ephesians 4:14

As we have already noted, false teaching abounds. And often it comes in the name of God. It can throw believers off balance and even lead some astray. The study of the Word informs the believer, stabilizing him against such error. (See Matthew 22:29.)

To Grow Up

▶Read 1 Peter 2:2

It's possible for Christians to be spiritually malnourished or immature. The cure is in the study of the Word. That is, we should have a normal and healthy appetite for God's Word, just like a baby has for milk. (Note: The reference to "milk" here is not in contrast to "solid food," as in 1 Corinthians 3:2 and Hebrews 5:12–14.)

If we are going to grow as Christians, we need to be nourished, and that nourishment comes from His Word. It is our food.

Through this study, you have already begun to spend time daily in God's Word. Ask God to help you maintain this practice and guide you to those verses you need.

Week Four: The Bible, The Basis of Our Belief

Day Six

Verses of the Bible I read:

What did they teach me?

What questions do I have?

What do I need to talk to God about?

Week Four: The Bible, The Basis of Our Belief

Day Seven

What has God shown me through His Word this week?

What questions do I have?

What changes have I seen in my life this week?

If I were asked why I read the Bible, what would I say?

Week Five: Prayer, Praise, and Worship

BIBLE VERSES TO MEMORIZE:

1 John 1:9—"If we confess our sins, he is faithful and just and will forgive us our sins."

Romans 12:1—"I urge you, brothers, in view of God's mercy, to offer your bodies as living sacrifices, holy and pleasing to God—which is your spiritual worship."

Week Five: Prayer, Praise, and Worship

Day One: The How and Why of Prayer

Key Verses: Daniel 6:10; Matthew 6:5–6; Mark 14:38; Philippians 4:6; Hebrews 11:6; James 5:13; 1 John 1:9

You know by now that communication with God is two-way. We have been studying about how God can speak to us through His Word, but we can also come to Him in prayer and in praise. (This aspect of the Christian life is sometimes identified as the church's ministry to the Lord.)

To Be Spiritually Fit

▶Read Mark 14:38

Temptation is a fact of spiritual life. If you are to resist it, you must be a person of prayer, to make your spirit strong and alert. Otherwise, your natural desires may cause you to give in. (See Galatians 5:16–17.)

To Handle Trouble

▶Read James 5:13

A crisis can make us lose our heads, to grow discouraged, to worry. But the one response to problems that will always get positive results is prayer. So James says if anyone is in trouble, he should pray about the matter—not worry.

On the other hand, if you aren't facing problems, you probably know people who are. Pray for them. Jesus prayed for His disciples; He even prayed for you and me (John 17:20). Paul prayed for others (Colossians 1:9) and asked others to pray for him (Colossians 4:3–4). This is one way we carry each others burdens (see Galatians 6:2).

To Be Obedient

▶Read Philippians 4:6

Like Jesus, Paul did not suggest prayer, he commanded it. This tells us that prayer is vital to the believer—a matter of spiritual life and death. At the same time, prayer is tied to practical matters, as Paul (and James) indicates.

To Receive Forgiveness

▶Read 1 John 1:9

Spiritual life from God begins through a prayer for forgiveness. John teaches that we will continue to have a need for forgiveness. So as soon as you recognize your offense, pray for forgiveness.

Persistence in Prayer

▶Read Daniel 6:10

Daniel's prayer life did not consist merely of praying at mealtimes and before bed; he diligently sought the Lord throughout the day—even though he faced persecution as an exile in Babylon. What a great example! (See also Luke 18:1.)

Praying Sincerely

▶Read Matthew 6:5–6

Describe, in your own words, Jesus' teaching about prayer.

_____

_____

_____

_____

Praying in Faith

▶Read Hebrews 11:6

Prayer is not an empty ritual. It is a matter of faith—believing, trusting—in God. "Without faith it is impossible to please God," says Hebrews. (See Mark 9:21–27.)

Do you have needs today that you want to take before God? Now is the time to do just that. Remember, He loves you and already has the answer to every situation.

Week Five: Prayer, Praise, and Worship

Day Two: Why Praise?

Key Verses: 1 Thessalonians 5:18; James 5:13; 1 Peter 2:9

Praise is the spoken declaration of God's glory. It is directed to Him alone, though often we can glorify Him by allowing others to hear us offer praise (see Psalm 22:22). Throughout the Bible, praise is an acknowledgment of God as the Creator and man as the created (see Psalm 8).

Chosen to Praise

▶Read 1 Peter 2:9

Write this verse.

_____

_____

_____

_____

_____

Just as in the Old Testament God chose the Jews to be His people, in the New Testament He chose the Christian: We have been chosen to offer God praise. In 2:5 Peter says we offer "spiritual sacrifices" (in contrast to literal sacrifices) to God. In 2:9, people seem to be the audience: We "declare" God's praises so others get the message. Note that this verse also tells what God has done and why He is worthy of praise. (See Psalm 9:11.)

To Express Well-being

▶Read James 5:13

If you feel good, let God know. That is, respond to the impulse to give God thanks for your happiness or satisfaction. If the weather makes you feel good, thank God. If finishing a task makes you feel relief, praise God. If seeing a friend makes you feel warm inside, bless God. James says "every good and perfect gift is ... from the Father" (1:17). So do the natural thing and express appreciation to Him for everything good in your life.

Praise can take the form of thanks for what God has done, but it also includes a recognition of who He is. Tell God how much you love Him and thank Him for His fellowship with you, then praise Him because of who He is, the great God of all things.

To Do God's Will

▶Read 1 Thessalonians 5:18

Paul told the believers at Philippi that he had "learned to be content whatever the circumstances" (Philippians 4:11). Things may change, but God doesn't. Paul went a step further with the believers at Thessalonica, telling them to *"give thanks in all circumstances."* (Not "for" all circumstances, but "in" all circumstances.) For it is God's will that His people have hearts of gratitude, in contrast to unbelievers, whose lives are usually marked by ingratitude (see Romans 1:21).

Week Five: Prayer, Praise, and Worship

Day Three: Devotion—An Attitude of Life

Key Verses: Psalm 51:17; Daniel 3:16–18; Micah 6:8; Mark 12:30; Romans 12:1; 1 Thessalonians 5:17

Prayer and praise ideally grow out of our devotion to God—which is more of an attitude than an activity. And why shouldn't we become devoted to God? After all, "while we were still sinners, Christ died for us" (Romans 5:8).

Obeying the Greatest Commandment

▶Read Mark 12:30

The *Guinness Book of World Records* is popular because

people like to know about the greatest, the most, the highest, etc. Someone questioned Jesus along the same lines: What was the "most important" commandment? Jesus didn't have to think about it; it was right there in the Old Testament (Deuteronomy 6:5)—Love God with everything in you, body and soul, heart and mind. When we are obeying that commandment, we are living a life of devotion.

Become a *Living* Sacrifice

▶Read Romans 12:1

Under the Old Testament Law, animal sacrifices were offered to God in worship. Paul wanted his readers to see themselves as sacrifices, *living* sacrifices, presenting their whole lives to God as their "spiritual act of worship." Learn how to do "whatever you do . . . in the name of the Lord Jesus" (Colossians 3:17). (See Hebrews 13:15–16.)

Walk Humbly with God

▶Read Psalm 51:17; Micah 6:8

Solomon wrote that pride goes before destruction (Proverbs 16:18). The Psalmist said that God knows the proud at a distance (Psalm 138:6). Pride separates us from God; humility brings us into fellowship with Him.

An Attitude of Prayer

▶Read 1 Thessalonians 5:17

Paul is not telling us that we are to spend every moment of every day on our knees praying; he is telling us we should always be in an attitude of prayer, faithful and ready to pray. Prayer should be a common part of our lives.

Be Loyal to God No Matter the Outcome

▶Read Daniel 3:16–18

A child cannot always understand the ways of his parents. For example, he might question their love for him when he has to visit the dentist. The three young Jews facing the fiery furnace may have had similar misgivings. Nevertheless, they recognized that God is in control—and left it at that. Whatever happened to them, they would remain true to God.

Week Five: Prayer, Praise, and Worship

Day Four: Man Proposes, God Disposes

Key Verses: Psalm 27:13–14; Jeremiah 10:23; Matthew 8:2–3; 26:42; John 16:24; 2 Corinthians 12:7–9; James 4:2–3;13–15

An old debate in Christianity is God's sovereignty versus human freedom to choose. For example, will God do nothing in people's lives unless they make the right choices, in this instance, to pray? Or will God carry out all His plans regardless of what people do?

In reply, someone once said, "Man proposes, but God disposes." That is at least a part of the Bible's answer. (See Proverbs 16:9; 19:21.)

Don't let the debate worry you. Pray and trust God: "He is the Rock, his works are perfect, and all His ways are just" (Deuternomy 32:4).

God Knows Best

▶Read Jeremiah 10:23

Jeremiah was a devout prophet of God. Yet he realized man's limitations, including his own, for controlling his future. Here he acknowledges that to God, so that He might in some way take it into account as He judges His people as a nation for their sin.

In Jesus' Name

▶Read John 16:24

Jesus was not offering a magical formula when He said to pray in His name (which is how the seven sons of Sceva [Acts 19:13–16] thought). To pray in Jesus' name is to pray according to who He is and what He stands for, not simply according to what we want.

Not My Will

▶Read Matthew 26:42; James 4:13–15

Here Jesus offers an example of how to pray: We pray that our wills and God's agree. And if they do not, we back off with our wishes, our desires, our will, and say, "Your will be done." James warns us about setting out on our own, without any acknowledgment that God is in charge of our lives.

Yes

▶Read Matthew 8:2–3

Sometimes you will get from God just exactly what you ask for. Be sure to thank God for it (see Luke 17:17–18). Allow it to humble you as well. You are in harmony with the great God of the universe (see Psalm 8:1,4).

No

▶Read 2 Corinthians 12:7–9; James 4:2–3

No is a possible answer to prayer. James identifies one reason for a negative answer: self-indulgence. The Psalmist identifies another: "If I had cherished sin in my heart, the Lord would not have listened" (Psalm 66:18).

Paul had a unique experience of no for an answer to prayer. Actually he got more than a no. God told him, " 'My grace is all you need' " (Today's English Version). We may not need deliverance either; instead we may need to recognize that God's grace can make us equal to the situation.

Wait

▶Read Psalm 27:13–14

God has His own timetable and His own agenda. Sometimes divine intervention in our lives is simply a matter of His timing: having a flat tire and missing a car pileup, facing an unanticipated expense and then getting money in the mail. (See, for example, John 11:3–6.)

Week Five: Prayer, Praise, and Worship

Day Five: Corporate Praise

Key Verses: 1 Kings 8:27; Psalms 50:23; 95:6–7; 100:4; Isaiah 66:1–2

In addition to the praise that we bring to the Lord individually, we offer praise collectively when we come together anywhere as the body of Christ, when we gather in His name (see Matthew 18:20). Let's see what the Bible tells us about these special times.

The Call to Worship

▶Read Psalm 95:6–7

God desires that His people come together for worship and

praise (see also Hebrews 10:25). If you have yet to make church attendance a regular part of your life, take the admonition of this verse and become a part of a congregation. If you already are a part, join your voice with theirs in praising the Lord.

What are we to do when we gather as God's people? Listen to His Word and praise Him. Every time you attend church, remind yourself that a primary reason for such a gathering is to praise the Lord. (See Psalm 96:8–9.)

The Place of Worship

▶Read 1 Kings 8:27; Isaiah 66:1–2

God does not live in buildings; He lives in people. Thus God can be worshipped by His people anywhere. The early Jewish Christians used the synagogues until they were no longer welcome. Then they used their own homes. Buildings set aside exclusively for meetings of the church (that is, God's people) did not come until much later. When the Bible uses the word "church" it means the people of God. For example, when Jesus said, "I will build my church," He was talking about people, not buildings.

Reason for Worship

▶Read Psalms 50:23; 100:4

Here the Psalmist encourages us to praise the Lord. Why? Read verse 5 of chapter 100.

_____

_____

_____

In Psalm 50:23 God speaks of showing us his salvation. That is reason enough to praise Him, but you will learn more reasons as you grow in God.

We will be discussing the church more fully later, but it is important that we recognize that God has ordained praise as an important part of the church. If you have questions about how to praise the Lord with others, discuss it with your pastor. Most importantly, keep praising the Lord.

Week Five: Prayer, Praise, and Worship

Day Six

Verses of the Bible I read:

What did they teach me?

What questions do I have?

What do I need to talk to God about?

Week Five: Prayer, Praise, and Worship

Day Seven

What has God shown me through His Word this week?

What questions do I have?

What changes have I seen in my life this week?

If someone asked me why I pray, what would I answer?

Week Six: The Kind of Conflict We're In

BIBLE VERSES TO MEMORIZE:

1 John 4:4—*"The one who is in you is greater than the one who is in the world."*

2 Corinthians 10:4—*"The weapons we fight with . . . have divine power to demolish strongholds."*

Week Six: The Kind of Conflict We're In

Day One: Cosmic Warfare

Key Verses: Zechariah 4:6; 2 Corinthians 10:4; Ephesians 6:12

Although you're still human, you have, nevertheless, entered the realm of the spirit by being born again: You are alive to God. You are also alive to His enemy. You have entered a realm of cosmic proportions; your participation has cosmic significance. But don't let that intimidate you. Simply become sensitive to God's Spirit, and He will make you "more than a conqueror" (see Romans 8:37).

The Real Battle

▶Read Ephesians 6:12

This verse tells us that our true enemy is unseen; the ways of Satan are deceptive and hidden. Nevertheless, you can become aware of them (see 2 Corinthians 2:11). To understand that a war is raging in the spiritual realm is to gain an understanding of what you face each day.

Your real battle takes place in a spiritual realm against supernatural forces. That is, human opponents are often simply inspired by an unseen evil much greater than themselves. In this respect, other people are not your real problem; they are Satan's victims and he is using them. (See 2 Corinthians 4:4).

The Real Weapons

▶Read 2 Corinthians 10:4

What can you do in the face of evil, especially in places that seem beyond your influence? Paul, who faced human authority in high places, reassures us that we have weapons "that have _____ _____" to "demolish strongholds." Though he was often in a prison cell, his prayers were unbounded: Evil forces in the spirit world must have considered Paul always armed and dangerous. You can be regarded the same way as you develop your prayer life. (See Ephesians 6:13–18.)

" 'By My Spirit,' says the Lord"

▶Read Zechariah 4:6

Zechariah was called by God to motivate His people (back from exile in Babylonia) to rebuild the Temple. But Zechariah was not a king like David or Solomon, who could command fabulous materials and numerous workers to get the job done. Then came God's word of encouragement: The job would be done through the strength of the Spirit (not through natural resources), which is how believers still win their battles.

Week Six: The Kind of Conflict We're In

Day Two: Know the Enemy

Key Verses: Zechariah 3:1; Matthew 13:38–39; 1 Peter 5:8

The evil forces in this world that fight against the Christian and his desire to live for God are led by Satan. In order to fully understand the conflict we are in, we must recognize the author of the conflict.

Like a Roaring Lion

▶Read 1 Peter 5:8

Why does Peter tell believers to be alert?

_____

_____

The first step in dealing with and defeating the enemy is realizing that he is always on the prowl for unsuspecting souls.

The second step (according to verse 9) is to "_____" him. Do not give in. Do not be frightened. "The one who is in you is greater than the one who is in the world" (1 John 4:4).

The Accuser

▶Read Zechariah 3:1

What is Satan doing in this verse?

___

Did you know that he is doing this today as well? He slanders you before God, bringing one accusation after another. But those accusations are no threat because of Jesus' sacrifice for us. Satan accuses, but Jesus steps forward and shows the Father His nail-scarred hands, which show His sacrifice and the defeat of Satan.

The Sower of Evil

▶Read Matthew 13:38–39

Satan may be defeated when he works his evil against God's children, but he has much success against the children of this world. This story tells us that the evil one, Satan, sows his seed among the seed sown by God. Not until the day of judgment will the sorting occur, so "let us not become weary in doing good, for at the proper time we will reap a harvest if we do not give up" (Galatians 6:9).

In your prayer, ask God to help you become aware of the enemy and his ways so you won't be deceived.

Week Six: The Kind of Conflict We're In

Day Three: Know Where the Battle Is

Key Verses: Matthew 15:18–20; Romans 8:5–8; Galatians 5:16–17

In most wars, where opposing armies meet, a line is formed called the front. Usually, the farther back from the front line a person is, the greater his safety. In spiritual warfare, no such front line exists; it is not on the mission field or in the inner city. Satan's forces bring the battle to each believer. In a sense, we are surrounded, and our minds and hearts are the objective.

The Conflict of Our Natures

▶Read Galatians 5:16–17

Before you became a Christian, you may not have been aware of any conflict within yourself, perhaps because you simply followed your sinful nature. (See John 8:44 and 1 Corinthians 6:9–11.)

But when a person becomes a Christian, he is given a new nature, and although his sinful nature is still with him, he can resist it. He now can choose the Spirit's options.

In Romans 6:8–14, Paul wrote of considering ourselves "dead to sin but alive to God in Christ Jesus" (v. 11). However, considering ourselves "dead to sin" must be developed as a disposition, for it is not a once-and-for-all decision. So keep making that decision.

The Conflict in the Mind

▶Read Romans 8:5–8

The conflict between our natures is connected to the conflict in our minds. If we have a mind-set for God, we will usually choose those things that please God and strengthen our spirits. But if we put our minds at the disposal of the enemy, where will our thoughts ultimately lead us? (See verse 6.) _____

The Conflict of the Heart

▶Read Matthew 15:18–20

A person can have a very religious appearance, but what matters to God is the heart behind that appearance. Satan may even help a person "keep up appearances," as long as he has the person's heart; it is a prize of spiritual warfare. That's why Solomon wrote, "Above all else, guard your heart, for it is the wellspring of life" (Proverbs 4:23). (See also Colossians 3:1.)

Losing these battles doesn't mean the war is over, so don't stack arms. John tells us we have a great High Priest, our Lord Jesus; if we will confess our sin to Him, He will intercede for us before the Father. (See 1 John 1:9.)

Living a spiritual life means a battle, one that will be fought every day of our lives. Spend time each day asking God to help win the day's battles. That's a safe way to start every day.

Week Six: The Kind of Conflict We're In

Day Four: Know Your Commander in Chief

Key Verses: Matthew 28:18; Romans 14:8–9; Colossians 1:18; 1 John 4:4

You have been encouraged to get to know Christ better and better. For the spiritual conflict you are in, you should recognize Him as your Commander in Chief. He has won the final victory for us and leads us in the mopping up phase of the conflict.

All Authority Is His

▶Read Matthew 28:18

The typical rabbi of Jesus' day quoted other rabbis to reinforce his teaching. Jesus' teaching didn't need such reinforcement, for He taught "as one who had authority" (Matthew 7:29). In fact, He has "all authority." It was given to Him by His Father. Thus He is in a position to commission us to do His will, overcoming evil.

Supreme Head of All Things

▶Read Colossians 1:18

God's Son, Jesus Christ, was commissioned to come to earth to break the back of evil and sacrifice himself for mankind. He fulfilled His mission perfectly. So God gave Him supremacy. According to this verse, Jesus was given supremacy over how much? _____

Keep that in mind when you experience temptation or come up against evil. Turn to your Commander in Chief; He'll see you through. For if you stand firm against the devil's temptation, he will flee. If you fight against him, he will run.

Lord of the Dead and the Living

▶Read Romans 14:8–9

Death frightens many people. Paul called it "the last enemy" (1 Corinthians 15:26); it will be eliminated at the final judgment of all things (see Revelation 20:14). However, Jesus has already settled the matter by coming back from the dead, "so, whether we live or die, we belong to the Lord."

Resident in You

▶Read 1 John 4:4

Here is a profound and humbling truth: You and I are indwelt by God's Spirit. John's readers knew that too. But maybe they felt surrounded by the "many false prophets" (v. 1) and "the spirit of the antichrist" (v. 3). In any case, John felt he needed to make a point of the comparative strength of the Spirit in them and the spirit at large in the world.

How do the strengths of the Spirit in you and the spirit in the world compare?

_____

_____

Let that truth encourage you. Whatever you face, you are equal to it because you house the Spirit of God.

Week Six: The Kind of Conflict We're In

Day Five: Know the End

Key Verses: 2 Thessalonians 2:8; Hebrews 2:14; Revelation 20:10

A number of events will occur as God wraps up His plans for mankind (as far as we know them from the Bible). They are spoken of as the last things. Here again, God is in charge and He "knows those who are his" (2 Timothy 2:19). You don't need to let anything happening in this world today shake you. In God you're secure.

Overthrow of the Lawless One

▶Read 2 Thessalonians 2:8

According to this verse, how will Jesus overthrow the "lawless one"?

_____

Which means it will not take much effort on His part. (See Isaiah 11:4.)

Death Destroyed

▶Read Hebrews 2:14

By Jesus' death, He has assured the ultimate death of Satan, the one who beguiles people into sin, bringing them under its penalty—death (thus having "the power of death"). Jesus himself is "the resurrection and the life" and said, "He who believes in me will live, even though he dies" (John 11:25).

The Devil Put in His Place

▶Read Revelation 20:10

We win! A day will come when Jesus, our Lord and Savior, will bring Satan to his ultimate defeat. Never again will he trouble God's children, but he will spend all eternity in everlasting torment. And we know that we will spend all eternity in the glorious presence of God Almighty.

Week Six: The Kind of Conflict We're In

Day Six

Verses of the Bible I read:

What did they teach me?

What questions do I have?

What do I need to talk to God about?

Week Six: The Kind of Conflict We're In

Day Seven

What has God shown me through His Word this week?

What questions do I have?

What changes have I seen in my life this week?

If I were asked to explain the battle between my old life of sin and my new life in Christ, I would say . . .

Week Seven: Living Life by the Spirit

BIBLE VERSES TO MEMORIZE:

John 14:16—"I will ask the Father, and he will give you another Helper . . . to stay with you forever" (Good News Bible).

2 Timothy 1:7—"The Spirit that God has given us does not make us timid; instead, his Spirit fills us with power, love, and self-control" (Good News Bible).

Week Seven: Living Life by the Spirit

Day One: Jesus' Promise of the Holy Spirit

Key Verses: John 7:38–39; 14:16,26; 16:13; 1 Corinthians 6:19

When Jesus was preparing for His return to heaven, He knew His disciples would have to face the struggles of life without Him. At the same time, He knew that His Father had never planned for them to be without His presence. So Jesus promised His disciples He would not leave them like orphans. Although Jesus would be leaving, something wonderful was in store for the disciples . . . and for us: the Holy Spirit. Let's see exactly what this Holy Spirit would do.

Another Helper

▶Read John 14:16

The Greek language of the New Testament indicates Jesus said in effect that the Holy Spirit was "another" like himself—

not "another" in the sense of a different kind. The Holy Spirit would take Jesus' place among them. The Holy Spirit would be to the disciples what Jesus himself had been (fulfilling Jesus' promise to return to the disciples [John 14:18]).

The Greek word the Gospel writer used to identify the Holy Spirit in coming to the disciples was *paraclete*. In comparing versions of the New Testament, you will find a number of different translations of that word: "Advocate," "Counselor," "Comforter," "Helper." Dr. Stanley Horton in *What the Bible Says About the Holy Spirit* focuses on a combination of "Helper" and "Teacher."

Another Teacher

▶Read John 14:26; 16:13

Among other things, the Holy Spirit is the Teacher of Truth. Just as Jesus had taught the disciples, so the Holy Spirit would teach them.

In those times when the disciples needed to apply Jesus' teaching, the Holy Spirit would remind them of what Jesus had taught them. It would be like having Jesus with them again.

A Growing Presence

▶Read John 7:38–39; 1 Corinthians 6:19

Paul tells us that "your body is a _____ of the Holy Spirit, who is _____ you." Did you know that? God's Spirit came into you when you gave Jesus your heart. And He lives in you. But in John, Jesus promised a fullness of His Spirit, a baptism, which follows being born of the Spirit. In other words, there's more: The Holy Spirit will come to you as He came to the disciples after Jesus had left.

The Bible has a lot to say about the Holy Spirit; some Christian groups tend to overlook it. Throughout this week you will be examining that material. Today ask the Holy Spirit to guide your understanding so that you can know His presence in your life in a powerful way.

Week Seven: Living Life by the Spirit

Day Two: The Holy Spirit—God's Spirit

Key Verses: Luke 11:13; 24:49; Acts 1:8; 6:3,8

Who is the Holy Spirit? He is God. Just as Jesus is God, so

the Holy Spirit is God. The Bible tells us that God has manifested himself as God the Father, God the Son (Jesus), and God the Holy Spirit (see Matthew 28:19). It is this third member of the Trinity that we are considering here.

A Ready Gift from God

▶Read Luke 11:13

Yesterday you saw that Jesus had promised to send the Holy Spirit to the disciples. This verse also tells us that the Holy Spirit is God's gift to us. In effect, God has given us himself: His Son as our Savior and His Holy Spirit as our Helper. A person cannot give anything greater than himself.

A Command from the Son

▶Read Luke 24:49

To Jesus, the fullness of the Holy Spirit was not optional for His disciples. His words of instruction were to "_____ in the city until you have been clothed with power from on high."

Just as Jesus did not begin his ministry until the Spirit came on Him (see Luke 3:21–23), so the disciples were to wait for the anointing and empowering of the Holy Spirit before they undertook the work Jesus commissioned them to do.

Empowering for Service

▶Read Acts 1:8; 6:3,5,8

When God commissions us to do His work, He enables us. Note the association of power and being filled with the Spirit in these verses. Certainly a power beyond the comprehension of mankind is the power of the Holy Spirit. In each of these instances, power and fullness of the Spirit were present in the disciples so they could serve God and people. And that power and fullness is for today, for you.

We have already seen that the Holy Spirit guides us, leads us, and gives us power. We have also seen how much Jesus wants us to have the Holy Spirit. Now talk to God and ask Him to give you the power you need to serve in the way He wants you to.

Week Seven: Living Life by the Spirit

Day Three: The Day of Pentecost

Key Verses: Joel 2:28; Acts 2:1–4,38–39

Not long after Jesus returned to heaven, the promised Holy Spirit came to the disciples. It was an unusual event (then as well as now). Take the time to read Acts 2, noting the crowd's reaction and Peter's explanation.

The Prophecy of the Spirit's Coming

▶Read Joel 2:28

Many portions of the Bible contain prophecies that were later fulfilled. The prophet Joel preached and prophesied at least six centuries before Jesus was born.

What exciting prophecy does he give here?

_____

_____

The Fulfillment of the Prophecy

▶Read Acts 2:1–4

The Day of Pentecost was a harvest festival that came fifty days (*Pentecost* means "fiftieth") after the Passover Feast. It occurred about ten days after Jesus returned to heaven. Peter identifies the events on this particular Day of Pentecost as the fulfillment of the verse in Joel. God was pouring His Spirit on His people.

What supernatural aspects of this event are described in these verses?

1. _____

2. _____

3. _____

Receiving the Holy Spirit

▶Read Acts 2:38–39

So how does one receive this great blessing? Peter told the

people of that day that they needed to repent and be baptized in water and then they would be baptized in the Holy Spirit. In other words, it is a repentance that leads to salvation. Since you have already given your life to Jesus and received salvation, He is ready to fill you with the Holy Spirit.

You may have a great many more questions about the baptism of the Holy Spirit; if you do, talk with your pastor or a Spirit-filled friend. He can be specific in answering your concerns and praying with you that you might be filled with the Holy Spirit. Today thank God for this blessing and ask Him to lead you so that you might receive.

Week Seven: Living Life by the Spirit

Day Four: Power for Witnessing

Key Verses: Matthew 10:16–20; Acts 4:8–10,31; 19:8

The last two days this week, we want to discuss why God has sent this power. Today we will look at that power given for witnessing. To be a witness means to have seen something firsthand and then relate it to another. We are witnesses of Jesus Christ as we tell others what we have found in Him. We are also witnesses when we live our lives so that others can see that we have witnessed the Son of God (see John 13:35).

Facing Opposition

▶Read Matthew 10:16–20

One of the fundamental purposes of the baptism of the Holy Spirit is strength and wisdom for witnessing. Jesus was aware of the opposition His disciples (now as well as then) would face. The Early Church members needed the power of the Holy Spirit to overcome their enemies and stand firm with the message of the gospel. In today's world, opposition to our witness is usually more subtle—but it is still opposition of the enemy; we need the Spirit as much as Jesus' first disciples did.

The Example of the Disciples

▶Read Acts 4:8–10,31

Because of the fullness of the Spirit in their lives, Peter and John were able to stand firm and confound those who fought against them.

Others in the Early Church would be put to death for their

faith. Stephen and James were both killed in their attempt to spread the gospel. The early Christians saw this difficult time and prayed that God would somehow help them stand firm. The Holy Spirit filled them, and the Bible tells us that they spoke the Word of God with boldness. We, too, need this boldness as we witness for the Savior.

The Example of Paul

▶Read Acts 19:8

As an apostle, Paul sought to evangelize the Gentile world; his ministry was often marked by the boldness of the Holy Spirit. This challenges us today.

Can you think of five friends who need to accept Jesus Christ as you did?

_____

_____

_____

_____

_____

Ask God to give you the power you need to be His witness to them.

Week Seven: Living Life by the Spirit

Day Five: Power for Daily Living

Key Verses: 2 Timothy 1:7; Galatians 5:16; Romans 8:9–13

The Holy Spirit, as we have said, brings power from the throne of God. That power gives us strength to stand firm and proclaim the salvation of God in the middle of difficulties. It also gives us the strength we need to live daily for the Lord.

Qualities of God's Spirit

▶Read 2 Timothy 1:7

Timothy seems to have lacked confidence, perhaps because as a leader he was self-conscious about his youth (see 1 Timothy

4:12). Paul encouraged him by elaborating on the kind of Spirit God gives us. What three characteristics of God's Spirit did Paul identify?

_____

_____

_____

A Result of Obeying the Spirit

▶Read Galatians 5:16

Paul offered to the Galatian believers a kind of if/then proposition about living an overcoming life (for example, see this verse in the New English Bible): If they would allow the Spirit to guide their lives, what would be the result concerning their sinful natures?

_____

The kind of Greek verb Paul uses has to do with habitual conduct, not just a one time occurrence. That is, day by day we say yes to God's Spirit, to the good, the right, and the wholesome; perhaps that is why Paul speaks of such a life, literally, as a "walk" in the Spirit rather than a "stand" in the Spirit.

The Potential of Living by the Spirit

▶Read Romans 8:9–13

This is one of the most important passages of the Bible for our daily walk with Christ. Once we learn that we now have a say in how we act and react, we are on our way to an overcoming life, a life of refusing the devil, denying our sinful nature, and pleasing God.

That is, when we were dead in our sins, we were *slaves* to the deeds of our sinful nature (see Galatians 5:19–21). Even if we had been interested in living a righteous life, we could not have done so. The Law only tells a person he is a sinner; it does not provide the power to live righteously—God's Spirit does that. We now have that Spirit. Our task is to pay attention to that Spirit, learning what God's word teaches and doing it.

Praise the Lord for the presence of the Holy Spirit!

Week Seven: Living Life by the Spirit

Day Six

Verses of the Bible I read:

What did they teach me?

What questions do I have?

What do I need to talk to God about?

Week Seven: Living Life by the Spirit

Day Seven

What has God shown me through His Word this week?

What questions do I have?

What changes have I seen in my life this week?

If someone asked me about the purpose of the Holy Spirit, I would respond . . .

Week Eight: A Life of Love by Grace through Faith

BIBLE VERSES TO MEMORIZE:

Ephesians 2:8–9—"It is by grace you have been saved, through faith—and this not from yourselves, it is the gift of God—not by works, so that no one can boast."

Galatians 5:6—"The only thing that counts is faith expressing itself through love."

Week Eight: A Life of Love by Grace through Faith

Day One: Grace

Key Verses: Romans 5:1–2; Ephesians 2:6–7,8–9; Titus 2:11

Every Christian should thoroughly understand grace. A simplified definition is *God's Riches At Christ's Expense*. The following verses of the Bible will furnish a basis for a more adequate definition.

Grace Has Appeared

▶Read Titus 2:11

According to this verse, what has grace made possible?

Grace says that God takes the iniative: God looks for man, not vice versa.

Grace through Faith

▶Read Romans 5:1–2

God presents the opportunity to be saved and leaves it to a

person to take Him up on it. You have done that. By faith, by believing God's offer of salvation through His Son, you have entered the storehouse of God's grace, His generous favor. (See Ephesians 1:7 and Philippians 4:19.)

Not by Works

▶Read Ephesians 2:8–9

Some people have great difficulty accepting a gift; they feel they must in some way merit or pay for everything they get. When that thinking is applied to salvation, it is called works-righteousness. That is, the righteousness is earned or merited by good works. It is not a biblical doctrine. Grace is its opposite; it is the biblical doctrine. Remember its simplified definition (and see Romans 5:17).

Grace to Come

▶Read Ephesians 2:6–7

God did not make us a new creation in His Son by grace and then say, "You're on your own." God's generous favor continues all the way to heaven. As Hebrews 7:25 says, Christ "is able to save completely those who come to God through him."

Week Eight: A Life of Love by Grace through Faith

Day Two: What Is Faith?

Key Verses: John 20:29; 2 Corinthians 1:20; Hebrews 11:1,6; 1 John 5:4

We have touched on faith in previous weeks, because believing in God is where a person starts in his journey as a Christian: "Anyone who comes to [God] must believe he exists" (Hebrews 11:6). As we put our faith in God into practice, it will grow.

However, not everything taught about faith these days is in the Bible. We must proceed carefully on this topic.

Believing Is Seeing

▶Read John 20:29; Hebrews 11:1

The world says, "Seeing is believing." But Jesus said, "Blessed are those who have not seen and yet have believed." Jesus' blessing includes you. You have believed Jesus died and came back from the dead; that's part of the salvation message. And you've believed it even though you weren't there to witness it. That's faith!

Hebrews tells us that being certain of things we have not seen indicates faith. You believe that your sins are forgiven and that you will live for eternity with Jesus Christ in heaven—but have you ever actually seen someone go to heaven? No. But you believe because you have faith.

Believing on His Word

▶Read 2 Corinthians 1:20

Some Christians teach that if a person believes hard enough about something, that will make it so. Their emphasis is on the strength of one's faith. But it is the object of the Christian's faith that is important. (Remember day 4 of week 5, "Prayer, Praise, and Worship.")

We believe what Jesus has said in His Word. We can have confidence, or faith, in what He has promised, because we have faith in Him. You may want something badly, but believing or hoping does not cause it to happen. The promise of Christ and the work He does should be where we put our faith and trust.

Faith: The Winning Ingredient

▶Read 1 John 5:4; Hebrews 11:6

"Without _____ it is impossible to please God." If we cannot take God at His Word and trust Him, we cannot be pleasing to Him. He is worthy of our faith and trust because He is able to meet every need we have.

And it is our faith that _____ the world. This verse means that our confidence and trust in God will help us rise above the wickedness that would drag us down. Because I trust God, I know that He will see me through every struggle.

You will learn more about faith in the next few studies, but ask God to strengthen the faith you have now.

Week Eight: A Life of Love by Grace through Faith

Day Three: An Outpouring of Love

Key Verses: John 15:9; Romans 5:5; Ephesians 3:16–20; 1 Thessalonians 3:12

Certainly the Christian life should be marked by faith. It

should also be marked by love, for, as you have seen, "God is love" (1 John 4:8). However, John's emphasis here is on "God," not "love." Read it that way. In other words, God defines love, love does not define God. That means examining the Bible for its definition of the term, forgetting the romantic notion of love as a sentimental feeling that comes and goes. Christian love is, as one person put it, "an undefeatable attitude of goodwill" toward your fellowman, wanting nothing but God's best for him.

Love's Origin

▶Read John 15:9; Romans 5:5

Here we find the source of this special love. God the Father placed His love in Christ, His Son, who likewise places that love within each believer (which includes you). In other words, it is not a love we produce; it comes from God himself.

Rooted in Love

▶Read Ephesians 3:16–21

So great is Christ's love for us that it is beyond our comprehension. However, we are "rooted" and "established" in this love, so that we may be enabled to comprehend it. That is, we have the potential to understand and appreciate it; unbelievers do not.

Overflowing Love

▶Read 1 Thessalonians 3:12

Who is to be the ultimate beneficiary of the love of God? _____ That's right! His love is to extend through us to the world. Paul tells us in this verse that he prays for God's people that they will allow the love of the Lord to increase in them so that they may show it to others.

If you are like most Christians, you are now a part of God's kingdom because someone shared that special love with you. On the following lines write a brief account of your salvation experience; be sure to include the names of those who were important in this great moment of your life.

_____

_____

_____

_____

_____

Make today's prayer time a special commitment to show God's love to those He brings your way. Ask for His strength to live for His glory.

Week Eight: A Life of Love by Grace through Faith

Day Four: Love in Practice

Key Verses: Deuteronomy 10:19; Matthew 22:39; John 13:35; 1 Peter 1:22

This study is a lesson in commands. The following verses contain God's commands through Christ and the apostles to love one another.

Love is the Sign of the Christian Community

▶Read John 13:35

Often the apostle John is referred to as the apostle of love. That's because God's love is a theme in everything he wrote. In his Gospel he includes Jesus' teaching that love is *the* sign of the Christian community. Few verses can be plainer than this one.

Pause now, and ask God to open your eyes to His love and to lead you in loving all other believers, especially those in your fellowship.

Love Sincerely and Deeply

▶Read 1 Peter 1:22

In this verse Peter, too, challenges us to love each other. One of the principal qualities of this love is revealed here. It is sincerity.

Love Others the Way You Love Yourself

▶Read Deuteronomy 10:19; Matthew 22:39

These verses give us an understanding of what God expects of us. He has a deep, sincere love for all people, and He wants you to have that same love (see John 3:16).

On the lines below, write the names of people you know who need God's love. Beside each name write a suggestion or two of how you might show His love to them. Before you make your list, ask God to open your mind to His understanding and your eyes to see what He sees.

_____:_____

_____:_____

_____:_____

_____:_____

_____:_____

Week Eight: A Life of Love by Grace through Faith

Day Five: Putting It All Together

Key Verses: Romans 8:35; 1 Corinthians 13:2; Galatians 2:20; 5:6

Now that we have begun to understand what faith and love mean to our new life in Christ, let's put it together with some very important Scriptures.

Faith without Love

▶Read 1 Corinthians 13:2

As you have seen, faith is important to the Christian life. In this verse, however, Paul puts it in perspective. No matter how great a person's faith, if love is not a part of it, what does Paul say that person amounts to? _____

No Separation

▶Read Romans 8:35

This verse presents a question that is answered in verses 38 and 39. Nothing can ever separate us from the love of our Lord Jesus. No matter what adversity we may face, we can be sure He will walk beside us and we can lean on Him.

That is one of the most exciting verses ever written! Hold on to its promise, for it will carry you through many a dark situation. To know that nothing the enemy may throw at you can force you from God's presence tells you that victory over every circumstance can be yours.

The Way to Show Your Faith

▶Read Galatians 5:6

The Galatian believers needed instruction about what was essential to their salvation. Some people were teaching them that they needed to practice the Law of Moses, especially circumcision. Paul, who had been a keeper of the Law, told them such things did not matter. What did he say mattered?

_____

Faith expresses itself in acts of love. (See 1 John 3:17–18.)

Christ in Us

▶Read Galatians 2:20

Finally, this verse puts it all together. I have laid myself aside and serve Christ because of my faith in Him, because He loved me. Therefore, my entire life flows from my faith and His love.

What a good time to thank the Lord for His grace and love. Also thank Him for bringing you to Him and strengthening your faith. Then ask Him to continue to help you learn to trust Him.

Week Eight: A Life of Love by Grace through Faith

Day Six

Verses of the Bible I read:

What did they teach me?

What questions do I have?

What do I need to talk to God about?

Week Eight: A Life of Love by Grace through Faith

Day Seven

What has God shown me through His Word this week?

What questions do I have?

What changes have I seen in my life this week?

If asked, how would I describe faith?

How would I define real love?

Week Nine: Becoming Like Jesus

BIBLE VERSES TO MEMORIZE:

2 Corinthians 3:18—"We, who with unveiled faces all reflect the Lord's glory, are being transformed into his likeness with ever-increasing glory, which comes from the Lord, who is the Spirit."

Galatians 5:22–23—"The fruit of the Spirit is love, joy, peace, patience, kindness, goodness, faithfulness, gentleness, and self-control."

Week Nine: Becoming Like Jesus

Day One: Following the Master

Key Verses: John 15:5; Luke 6:46; Matthew 16:24

Did you realize that your conversion is just the beginning of the life Jesus has called you to? You, as a child of God, must now pursue living in the manner God prescribes for those who would follow Him. That's what today's study is all about. Let's see what the Bible says.

Stay Connected to the Vine

▶Read John 15:5

Since Jesus is the vine and we are the branches, we must depend on Him so we might grow and produce fruit, that is, develop a godly life—become more like Jesus (see Matthew 3:8). Many times Christians forget this, losing sight of their need of Jesus. Don't let that happen to you. If you will learn the truth of this verse today, it will always be helpful to you in your Christian life.

Hold to Jesus' Teaching

▶Read Luke 6:46

If we confess Jesus as our Lord, what should that mean in our lives? Read John 8:31 and 2 Timothy 2:19 for further clues.

___

___

Put Jesus First

▶Read Matthew 16:24

This verse contains a supreme directive for the Christian life. Jesus tells us that if we truly would follow Him, we must deny ourselves. That means we must turn over to God our desires and ambitions and allow Him to direct us as He sees fit, so that we might serve God's kingdom not only where we may be needed, but also in the manner that pleases Him.

Certainly all there is to know about living like the Lord Jesus cannot be covered in one study—or a week of studies—so expect to keep learning about this topic throughout your life. For now, why not take time to ask God to help you become exactly what He wants and needs you to be? Then take time to thank Him for your new life and His promise to walk each step with you.

___

Week Nine: Becoming Like Jesus

Day Two: Called to Servanthood

Key Verses: Luke 22:25–26; John 12:24; 13:1–5; Philippians 2:5

As you come to understand more about God and His ways, you will find that the ways of the world are often just the opposite. In today's study, this opposition couldn't be clearer. For example, in our present society, as men and women try to move to the top of their careers, they often develop a lifestyle of self-centeredness; it seems that at the heart of almost every vocational situation, they have to ask questions like, "How does it affect me?" or "What's in it for me?"

Not so in the kingdom of God. We have been called to a different way. Let's see what the Bible tells us.

Don't Lord It over Others

▶Read Luke 22:25–26

Jesus tells us in this passage that the way to greatness in the Kingdom is through serving. You have already seen in a previous study that God wants us to deny ourselves. In practical terms, the serving of God and others is a principal way of doing just that.

But a servant? That's right! As a Christian, we have been called to a life of service to God and our fellowman. There's no greater calling.

Be Like the Greatest Servant

▶Read John 12:24; 13:1–5; Philippians 2:5

In this set of verses we are given Jesus as our example. Read John 13:6–9 and then imagine the reaction of the other disciples when Jesus washed their feet.

Write John 12:24 below.

_____

_____

_____

Do you understand this verse? The principle of life through death is seen in the plant world. If a seed were to resist that principle, it wouldn't be fruitful. Jesus gave the limit—His life; He asks the same of His followers.

Finally, Philippians 2:5 addresses this humility in a very special way. Why do we become servants? Because this was Jesus' approach to His earthly life, and the greatest worship we can show Him is to become just like Him.

Today, commit your prayer time to asking God to guide you in this new way of life. Tell Him that you are His willing servant, ready to be used by Him in whatever way He chooses. Then thank Him for the opportunity to be His servant.

Week Nine: Becoming Like Jesus

Day Three: Obedience, the Key

Key Verses: 1 Samuel 15:22; Matthew 7:24; Ephesians 4:1; Hebrews 5:8

When we discuss becoming like Jesus we must certainly focus on obedience. Some Christians fall into the error of thinking that obeying God is not that important. Don't believe it! Furthermore, true obedience is inward as much as it is outward (see, for example, Isaiah 29:13 and Matthew 21:28–32).

Jesus Learned Obedience

▶Read Hebrews 5:8

However this verse is explained, it contains the example of Jesus as He "learned obedience." This should help us see the importance of obedience in the life of the Christian. After all, Christians were first called "*followers* of [the] Way" (Acts 9:1–2 and 22:4). (To follow is to obey.)

God Prefers Obedience to Sacrifice

▶Read 1 Samuel 15:22

In Old Testament times, God instructed His people to offer sacrifices to cover their sins (a practice that foreshadowed Jesus' sacrifice of himself on the Cross). But God's people often forgot the purpose of the sacrifice; they would go through the motions and not truly be repentant of their sins. This verse indicates that God's priority is not sacrifice, but obedience. That's what He was trying to teach them. And it's what He wants to teach us.

Obedience Demonstrates Wisdom and Integrity

▶Read Matthew 7:24; Ephesians 4:1

Here, two more sets of instruction encourage us to be obedient to God. In Jesus' words, the obedient one is compared to a wise man who builds his house on a rock. What is Jesus' point?

_____

_____

Obedience to God is the only firm foundation to build our lives on.

What do you suppose Paul meant when he wrote to the believers at Ephesus to live a life worthy of the calling they had received? (Look at Colossians 1:9–14, noting verse 10, as well as Ephesians 4:2–3.)

_____

_____

_____

In a number of places in the Bible Jesus taught that a disciple's love was proved by his obedience (e.g., see John 15:14). If we are truly followers of God, we will show it by our obedience.

Week Nine: Becoming Like Jesus

Day Four: The Fruit of the Spirit

Key Verses: 1 Corinthians 13:4–7; Galatians 5:22,23; 2 Peter 1:5–7

How does the Bible describe a Christian? What are his traits? In these verses we have a profile of the character of the Christian—every Christian; this is the kind of person we should be. Notice that these qualities are not focused on *doing* for Christ, but *being* for Christ. Don't get them mixed up and major on doing something great for Christ and neglect being like Him.

Describing the Spirit-filled Believer

▶Read 1 Corinthians 13:4–7; Galatians 5:22,23; 2 Peter 1:5–7

List the marks of the life of a Spirit-filled child of God as mentioned in these three passages.

1 Corinthians	Galatians	2 Peter
Love:	_____	_____
_____	_____	_____
_____	_____	_____
_____	_____	_____
_____	_____	_____

(cont.)

1 Corinthians	Galatians	2 Peter
_____	_____	_____
_____	_____	_____
_____	_____	_____
_____	_____	
_____		
_____		
_____		
_____		

It's quite a list, isn't it? But God has promised us that He will help us to develop these traits in our lives if we will allow Him to work in us.

The Bible tells us that we are to become like Christ. Through the direction of the Holy Spirit and by His power we can. There are many different aspects to the Christian life, but we need to focus on becoming more like Christ. We may have great talents and abilities to do many things, but if we are not becoming more like Christ, then we will have no testimony, no witness, to our world.

The list above should be every Christian's goal, a goal that can be achieved through the power of God's Spirit in us. Spend your prayer time today asking God to work so that you might honor Him by becoming more like Him. God help us to grow in His image.

Week Nine: Becoming Like Jesus

Day Five: Transformed by His Power

Key Verses: Romans 8:29; 2 Corinthians 3:18; Galatians 4:19; Ephesians 4:13

Don't think you're on your own in becoming like Jesus. God is with you all the way: He has given you His Son, His Spirit is in you, His Word is at your fingertips, and He has made you a member of the body of Christ. Think about Romans 8:32.

God's Purpose for Us

▶Read Romans 8:29

According to this verse, what does God want to do with us who choose to believe in Him?

_____

God's purpose is to make us like His Son, a process that begins here and now—not when we get to heaven. The job gets finished in heaven, but it starts here.

Bearing the Image of Christ

▶Read Galatians 4:19

Paul was deeply concerned about the believers in Galatia: They were in danger of departing from the Christian faith that he had taught them. They were listening to teachers who were adding things that would lead them away from trusting only in Christ for salvation and developing Christ-like character.

Thus, any teaching that lessens the image of Christ in us is not completely Christian, for bearing His image should be the goal of every believer.

Transformed into His Likeness

▶Read 2 Corinthians 3:18

We are to be a reflection of God in this world. And we are—as we allow His Spirit to transform our attitudes, our behavior, and our outlook. Compare the above verse with Philippians 2:13. How are they alike? How are they different?

Similarities: _____

Differences: _____

According to this verse, does our transformation happen instantaneously or gradually? (Checking the phrasing of this verse in other versions of the Bible might be helpful in answering this question.) _____

Until We Become Mature

▶Read Ephesians 4:13

Note the context of this verse. Paul is talking about the body of Christ, the Church, and how God has placed certain members in the Body to help the rest of the members to achieve mature Christian character, "the whole measure of the fullness of Christ."

Here again we are not alone in our growth to maturity in Christ. Be certain that you find a place in the church to serve and be served. Don't make the mistake of trying to live your Christian life independent of other believers. If you do, your growth will be greatly hindered.

Week Nine: Becoming Like Jesus

Day Six

Verses of the Bible I read:

What did they teach me?

What questions do I have?

What do I need to talk to God about?

Week Nine: Becoming Like Jesus

Day Seven

What has God shown me through His Word this week?

What questions do I have?

What changes have I seen in my life this week?

What fruit should I be seeking to develop?

Week Ten: The People of God

BIBLE VERSES TO MEMORIZE:

1 Peter 2:10—"Once you were not a people, but now you are the people of God; once you had not received mercy, but now you have received mercy."

Ephesians 4:11–13—"It was [Christ] who gave some to be apostles, some to be prophets, some to be evangelists, and some to be pastors and teachers, to prepare God's people for works of service, so that the body of Christ may be built up until we all reach unity in the faith and in the knowledge of the Son of God and become mature, attaining to the whole measure of the fullness of Christ."

Week Ten: The People of God

Day One: What Is the Church?

Key Verses: 1 Corinthians 12:27; 1 Timothy 3:15; 1 Peter 2:9–10

One of the greatest blessings God has given to us is that of being made one of His people. This week's material looks at further ministry responsibilities of God's people. (You have already noted the church's ministry to the Lord, that is, worship.) Here we consider another of the overall ministries of the church: ministry to itself, that is, to believers.

God's People

▶Read 1 Peter 2:9–10

List the ways these verses describe God's people.

_____

_____

_____

_____

The question may be asked, Why all these terms? Why not just "people of God" all the time? Because each new term gives us some information about how God's people are related to each other and to God. (Remember, for example, the term "saint" from Day 2, Week 1?)

The Body of Christ

▶Read 1 Corinthians 12:27

Paul told the believers at Corinth that each of them made up the body of Christ. Note that in the very next verse, Paul writes, "And in the church . . ." From this we may conclude that the body of Christ and the church are synonymous. The Church of Jesus Christ is people who, just like you, have given their hearts to Him. We may sometimes think of the church as that large brick building with the cross on the front of it, but the term in the Bible is really to be defined as God's people. (Remember "The Place of Worship" on day 5 of week 5?)

God's Household

▶Read 1 Timothy 3:15

Paul writes to Timothy about conduct "in God's household." How does Paul further define this term?

_____

_____

Here again we see synonymous terms for the people of God. When you think of being in God's _household,_ what does that say to you?

_____

_____

Watch for other terms that identify God's people. Try to figure out why the writer used that particular term. That is one way to understand better your privileges and responsibilities as a child of God.

Week Ten: The People of God

Day Two: The Head of the Church

Key Verses: Ephesians 1:22; 4:11,15

Just as the New Testament writers used different terms to identify God's people, they also used different terms to identify Jesus Christ. You have seen that in a number of verses, for example, John 1:14 ("the Word"), Acts 7:56 ("Son of Man"), Revelation 22:13 ("Alpha and Omega").

For the success of any venture, it is essential to know who's in charge, the one with the final say. In Colossians 1:18 (Week 6, Day 4) you saw Christ as the head of all things. As you might expect, that includes the Church. The Bible makes that clear.

Head of Everything

▶Read Ephesians 1:22

Compare this verse with Colossians 1:18. How are they alike? How are they different?

Similarities: _____

Differences: _____

The Head of the Body

▶Read Ephesians 4:15

It may appear that the people who lead the worship or preach the sermons head up the church. Indeed, they are often called on to make vital decisions or give an authoritative challenge to God's people. But if the Church is the body of Christ (and a body has only one head), then it follows that that position ought to belong to _____.

Make sure you focus your attention, and especially your adoration, on Christ.

Jesus Christ, however, has given gifts of leadership to the church. Consider the verse below.

Ministering Pastors

▶Read Ephesians 4:11

This is one of your memory verses. It speaks of the various ministries Christ has put in the church. But notice who has put them there. The Head! That's right, it is Jesus Christ.

Understanding where people like your pastor fit in the picture is important. Pastors offer compassion, encouragement, direction, and challenge. They have been given that ministry of pastoring by Christ, they have been given the words of their message by Christ, and they have been given the strength to proclaim those words and live them by Christ. All that they have has been given them by Christ. So there is no room for idolizing or idealizing leaders (see 2 Corinthians 4:7); worship God alone, the giver of all good gifts (see James 1:17).

That would be a good way to close today's study. Just worship your Lord, thanking Him for making Christ the head of the Church and giving gifts, through His Son, for building you up.

Week Ten: The People of God

Day Three: "Body-building"

Key Verses: Acts 4:36; Romans 15:1–3; 2 Corinthians 12:19; Ephesians 4:11–12

An important part of being the body of Christ is investing ourselves in the lives of one another. The ministry of edification is the building up and encouraging of one another. This ministry is given a great deal of emphasis in God's Word.

Prepared for Service

▶Read Ephesians 4:11–12

You have looked at these verses before. As verse twelve indicates, God has gifted the Church to build one another up spiritually. God does not intend for us to be spiritual weaklings. He has given gifts to the Church for our encouragement, that we might grow to be what He wants us to become.

To Strengthen Others

▶Read 2 Corinthians 12:19

Here the apostle Paul explains himself to the Corinthians, telling them, "Everything we do . . . is for your _____"

Can you identify with Paul at this point?

A Good Example

▶Read Acts 4:36

This verse introduces a man named Joseph, whom the apostles had nicknamed Barnabas. What does Luke give as the meaning of that name? "_____"
Look up the following references—Acts 4:37; 9:26–27; 11:21–26; 15:36–40 (see also 1 Corinthians 9:6 and 2 Timothy 4:11)—and summarize the kind of person Joseph was to cause the apostles to nickname him Barnabas.

_____

_____

Oriented toward Others

▶Read Romans 15:1–3

Finally, we come to our responsibility—for this ministry of encouragement is not just for evangelists and pastors or men like Paul and Barnabas. Encouraging one another is for every member of the body of Christ. At times you may feel like you can't do a whole lot for God, but you can always speak an affirming word or simply give an encouraging look.

As you pray today, ask God to lead you to someone who needs encouragement. Then ask Him to give you the words or the means to be that "son of encouragement."

Week Ten: The People of God

Day Four: A Call to Ministry

Key Verses: 2 Corinthians 5:18–19; Galatians 6:9–10; Ephesians 4:11–13; 1 Thessalonians 5:14; Hebrews 13:1–2; 1 Peter 4:8–10

The life of the Church is filled with opportunities to serve God. The Bible describes some of those opportunities.

Ministries of the Church

▶Read Ephesians 4:11–13

This familiar passage tells how God has built His church.

He has called certain individuals to special ministries so that they might be used to bring growth to the lives of His people.

You may be familiar with some of the ministries mentioned. For example, the pastor is mentioned, and he or she has been given to your local church by God to help build up the people of God. From these verses what are the purposes of these ministries?

_____

_____

_____

_____

More Ministries

▶Read Galatians 6:9–10; 1 Thessalonians 5:14

Notice the responsibilities that each of us must bear within the church. What are some of the ministries at work in your church?

_____

_____

The Motivation of Ministry

▶Read Hebrews 13:1–2; 1 Peter 4:8–10

In keeping with Jesus' teaching (see John 13:34–35) and the character of God (see 1 John 4:16), the watchword of the Early Church became "love."

If we allow the love of God to flow through us to those in need, we can be certain that each need will be met.

Hospitality was important to the Early Church. In starting new churches, the apostles had to carefully appoint and instruct new leadership; they corresponded with and traveled to the many new churches spread about the region. Because commercial lodging was not very reputable, traveling Christians depended on their brothers and sisters in Christ for places to stay. Though commerical lodging has changed, the Bible's call for Christian hospitality has not.

Ministry of Reconciliation

▶Read 2 Corinthians 5:18–19

An additional area of ministry that is of great importance

is sharing the salvation message of Jesus Christ with those who have yet to accept Him. Throughout next week we will be discussing this in great detail.

What ministry can you become a part of? Why not make that the subject of your prayer time today? And remember, we do all these things because we love God and want to serve Him.

Week Ten: The People of God

Day Five: In Fellowship

Key Verses: Psalm 119:63; Acts 2:42; Romans 12:5; 1 John 1:7

Week 5 dealt with believers gathering to worship God. This week's material looks at another reason for gathering as believers—to fellowship. Fellowship is a significant aspect of believers getting together and it merits our attention. For example, what does the Bible teach about its practice?

The Basis of Our Fellowship

▶Read Psalm 119:63

This beautiful Psalm introduces the unique nature of the fellowship of God's people. This fellowship is not based on any similarities of personality or social status. That is what unbelievers base their fellowship on. According to this Psalm, the fellowship of God's people is based on a mutual desire to please God. Let's look at this a bit more closely.

Devotion for One Another

▶Read Acts 2:42; Romans 12:5

According to the verse in Acts, fellowship was very important to the early believers. After the Day of Pentecost, they "devoted" themselves to "the fellowship." They shared their material goods as well as their spritual wealth (see verse 45).

Romans describes a further aspect of this special relationship among Christians. Because we share the same faith and are a part of the body of Christ, we belong to each other. Not in the sense, of course, that we are one another's possession, but in the sense that we share a responsibility to love and nurture one another in the things of God.

Conduct for Maintaining Fellowship

▶Read 1 John 1:7

John says that fellowship is conditional. How must we be living our lives (i.e., our "walk") to have fellowship with one another?

_____

It is because of the righteousness of Christ and our desire to live holy lives that we keep in fellowship with each other.

Our brothers and sisters in Christ are a vital part of our Christian life. Can you think of certain ones that have already been a blessing to you in your new faith? Who are they, and why are they special?

_____:_____

_____:_____

_____:_____

Thank the Lord for them and determine that you will also become ministers to others so that they will be blessed.

Week Ten: The People of God

Day Six

Verses of the Bible I read:

What did they teach me?

What questions do I have?

What do I need to talk to God about?

Week Ten: The People of God

Day Seven

What has God shown me through His Word this week?

What questions do I have?

What changes have I seen in my life this week?

If someone asked me why I go to church, what would I say?

Week Eleven: The Church in Action—I

BIBLE VERSES TO MEMORIZE:

Matthew 28:19–20—"Go and make disciples of all nations, baptizing them in the name of the Father and of the Son and of the Holy Spirit, and teaching them to obey everything I have commanded you."

1 Corinthians 11:26—"Whenever you eat this bread and drink this cup, you proclaim the Lord's death until he comes."

Week Eleven: The Church in Action—I

Day One: Discipling/Teaching

Key Verses: Matthew 28:19–20; Acts 2:42; Philippians 4:9; 1 Timothy 4:13; 2 Timothy 2:2

Last week your study material centered on what the Bible says about the kind of people Christians ought to be. This week's material looks at the church's ordinances and practices.

Make Disciples

▶Read Matthew 28:19–20

Among Jesus' last words of instruction to His disciples is what has become known as the Great Commission: "Make disciples . . . teaching them to obey everything I have commanded you." No making of disciples can occur without teaching—and obedience to that teaching. It is good to invite a new convert to "experience" the Lord—but instructing and providing him an example is far better. For if he does not know what the Bible teaches and how he is supposed to live, he will have only his experience to go by. So if he wakes up with a headache or gets yelled at by his boss, he may think his "Christianity" is suspect. That is, his bad experience (with his body or his boss) may cause him to doubt his good experience (with the Lord).

New Testament Church Practice

▶Read Acts 2:42

This familiar verse describes the activity of the New Testament church shortly after Jesus returned to heaven. It devoted itself not only to fellowship, worship, and prayer, but to the apostles' _____ as well.

This indicates the disciples' (i.e., apostles) follow-through on Jesus' command.

Paul's Instruction and Example

▶Read Philippians 4:9; 1 Timothy 4:13; 2 Timothy 2:2

Almost a generation after the Church began, Paul discipled young churches as well as their leaders. The world would have us believe that it's okay if what a person says and what he does are two different things (particularly if he is a public official). The Bible teaches the opposite: What one says and does are to be one and the same. Otherwise Paul could not have written this verse to the believers at Philippi.

Writing the young church leader Timothy, Paul exhorted him to practice three things. Name them:

_____

_____

_____

In Paul's second letter to Timothy (which is his last New Testament writing—see 2 Timothy 4:6–8), Paul instructs Timothy to carry on the discipling he himself received from Paul (see 1 Corinthians 11:1). Here we see the continuing importance of a body of material to be learned, believed, and practiced.

Today let's thank God for the church and those special people He has given to teach and disciple us. And let's determine to be faithful so that we can in turn be an example others may follow.

Week Eleven: The Church in Action—I

Day Two: Water Baptism

Key Verses: Matthew 28:19; Acts 8:38; 10:47–48; Romans 6:3

Instituted by Jesus

▶Read Matthew 28:19

Here in the Great Commission, Jesus includes water baptism as an essential part of the work of the ministry. It is the command of our Lord, and we should certainly be obedient to Him. Notice how we are to be baptized: in the name of the Father, the Son, and the Holy Spirit. Just as when Jesus was baptized and all three persons of the Trinity were involved, so it is with our baptism.

Examples of Early Church Baptisms

▶Read Acts 8:38; 10:47–48

These two verses mention _____ in water. An important part of the life of the church is water baptism. In these instances, an Ethiopian court official and a Roman soldier (and his followers, including his family) are baptized in water after committing their lives to Jesus Christ and accepting His gift of forgiveness and salvation. Perhaps you wonder why they did this. The following verse helps answer that.

The Symbolism of Baptism

▶Read Romans 6:3

Water baptism is a symbol of what in the life of Christ?

_____

When you gave your life to Jesus Christ, your old self, your carnal nature, was to have been put to death. It was to be buried with its old ways, and the new life was to begin. Therefore, you symbolically "died with Christ" and were raised with Him to a new life.

Water baptism, then, is a symbol of what Jesus Christ has done inside you. It is also an opportunity to testify to others about what has taken place. In the life of the church, people are baptized in water to show what Christ has done in their hearts. It is a special moment to share. If you've not been baptized in water, talk to your pastor soon. This is very important.

Today, talk to the Lord about this baptism. Most of all, be thankful for the inside job he has done on you.

Week Eleven: The Church in Action—I

Day Three: Holy Communion

Key Verses: Luke 22:17–20; 1 Corinthians 10:16; 11:23–26

Another part of the life and ministry of the church is Holy Communion (also called the Lord's Supper). Some churches observe this weekly, others monthly. The Bible doesn't specify frequency, referring simply to "whenever" you do this. Communion is the paramount expression of fellowship in the church.

Symbols of the Sacrifice

▶Read Luke 22:17–20

Just a few hours before Jesus was taken into custody and put to death, He sat down with His disciples to celebrate the Feast of the Passover. The Passover was a remembrance of God's deliverance of Israel from Egypt (see Exodus 12).

After they had shared this special meal, Jesus took bread and wine and symbolically portrayed for His disciples what was about to happen in His life and in the plan of God. Jesus identified the bread as his _____ and the wine as his _____.

The bread and wine became symbols of His sacrifice for us: The bread was His body that would be broken; the wine was His blood that would be spilled. This is the "meal" Christians call the Lord's Supper, or Holy Communion.

A Proper Observance

▶Read 1 Corinthians 11:23–26

Many years after Jesus returned to heaven, Paul had to teach the believers at Corinth the proper observance of the Lord's Supper. He exhorted them to drop their self-centered approach and think instead of their fellow believers and the Lord Jesus.

Participants in His Sacrifice

▶Read 1 Corinthians 10:16

When believers rightly take the Lord's Supper, they do much more than just remember what Jesus has done for them. By faith—recognizing the reason for His broken body and spilled blood, trusting in His Atonement for sin—believers become not just bystanders in this sacred ceremony, but participants!

Today as you pray, again thank God for His gift of salvation. For we can never thank God enough for the wonderful blessings of His love and presence.

Week Eleven: The Church in Action—I

Day Four: Praying for the Sick

Key Verses: Isaiah 53:4; Matthew 4:23; 8:17; Mark 16:17–18; 1 Corinthians 12:7,9; James 5:14–15

One of the most familiar aspects of the ministry of Jesus and, consequently, the life of the Early Church was the concern and prayer for the healing of the sick. For some Christians today, this is a matter of controversy, but the Bible is quite clear in its teaching. Let's see what it says.

Jesus' Ministry of Healing

▶Read Matthew 4:23

"Jesus went throughout Galilee, _____ in their synagogues, _____ the good news of the kingdom, and _____ every disease and sickness among the people."

This verse identifies three aspects of Jesus' ministry. Today's verses, however, focus on the aspect of healing the sick. Everywhere Jesus went, the lame walked, the blind saw, the lepers were cleansed. But what of this ministry today?

His Healing Ministry Extended

▶Read Mark 16:17–18; 1 Corinthians 12:7,9; James 5:14–15

Jesus identified the signs that would accompany belief in Him. One of those signs is healing. Paul told the Corinthians that the Spirit gave gifts of _____ as a manifestation of His presence. Healing is a sign of the presence of the Holy Spirit.

Write James 5:14–15.

_____

_____

_____

_____

If we are sick, we should call for the elders, or leaders, of the church to come anoint us with oil and pray, and expect recovery.

Putting together what Jesus, Paul, and James taught, we can conclude that the ministry of healing is a continuing part of the church's activity today.

Healed by His Wounds

▶Read Isaiah 53:4; Matthew 8:17

In these verses we find why it is possible for us to be healed. When Jesus paid the penalty for sin, He also took the penalty that would remove sickness, for sickness as well as sin resulted from Adam's fall. If people can still be forgiven, they can still be healed.

To think what Jesus endured for us! As you pray, thank Him for His sacrifice, and tell Him that you trust Him with all your needs. He is worthy of that trust.

Week Eleven: The Church in Action—I

Day Five: What Is My Part?

Key Verses: Matthew 5:13–16; Acts 10:37–38; Ephesians 2:10; Colossians 1:9–10; 1 Timothy 6:18; Hebrews 10:24

Once we begin to understand what the church is all about, we want to find our special place of ministry so that we can begin to bear fruit for the kingdom of God. Let's see what advice and guidance God has for us.

The Life-style of Jesus

▶Read Acts 10:37–38

Here Peter summarizes the life of Jesus, and part of that summary is this: "He went around doing good." This description of Jesus' life should be fitting for every one of His followers. Note that we have the same resource: the anointing and empowerment of God's Spirit.

The Command of Jesus

▶Read Matthew 5:13–16

As we have noted, the Church is God's people. And God's people are God's people whether they are gathered or scattered. So here Jesus speaks of them as salt and light, in effect, scattered. From this verse, identify what Jesus means (1) by our being salt and light and thus (2) our effect on people:

1. _____

2. _____

The Will of God

▶Read Colossians 1:9–10; Ephesians 2:10

Part of God's will for His people is for them to do good works. Write down your reaction to these verses:

_____

_____

_____

However, do not think of yourself as working *for* God but rather working with Him. You are His coworker (see 1 Corinthians 3:9 and Mark 16:20). His burden is light (Matthew 11:30).

Good Deeds Encouraged

▶Read 1 Timothy 6:18; Hebrews 10:24

Putting these verses together, we see that encouragement to do good works should be coming from the pew as well as the pulpit.

Make your prayer: Lord, show me where I can be your servant, and use me!

Week Eleven: The Church in Action—I

Day Six

Verses of the Bible I read:

What did they teach me?

What questions do I have?

What do I need to talk to God about?

Week Eleven: The Church in Action—I

Day Seven

What has God shown me through His Word this week?

What questions do I have?

What changes have I seen in my life this week?

Already I have become involved in the ministry of the Church by . . .

Week Twelve: The Church in Action—II

BIBLE VERSES TO MEMORIZE:

Matthew 28:19–20—"Go and make disciples of all nations, baptizing them in the name of the Father and of the Son and of the Holy Spirit, and teaching them to obey everything I have commanded you."

2 Corinthians 5:18—"All this is from God, who reconciled us to himself through Christ and gave us the ministry of reconciliation."

Week Twelve: The Church in Action—II

Day One: The Ministry of Reconciliation

Key Verses: Matthew 28:19; 2 Corinthians 5:18; 1 Timothy 2:3–4; 2 Peter 3:9

In week 5 you considered the church's ministry to the Lord (that is, worship), and in week 10 you considered the church's ministry to itself (instruction and edification). This week's material presents the last of the church's three-fold ministry: ministry to the world (often identified as evangelism/missions).

Make Disciples of All Nations

▶Read Matthew 28:19

Sometimes we as Christians find it easy to sit back and enjoy the blessings of God, and we forget that God's intent is that His message be spread. Jesus' words here have been spoken of as the Great Commission, for He commissioned His disciples to spread the Good News to all lands.

This challenge is for you too. Have you had the opportunity to share your faith? God wants us to be available for sharing the gospel whenever He brings the opportunity. Remember Acts 1:8.

God Gives the Ministry

▶Read 2 Corinthians 5:18

Every Christian has been given the ministry of reconciliation. That does not necessarily mean travel to foreign countries; it does mean that Christians are to be reconcilers. Our message to unbelievers, wherever they are, is the same as Paul's to the Corinthians: "Be reconciled to God" (v. 20).

Accept this ministry from God and ask Him to help you practice it. It can start with family members, coworkers, classmates—anyone who is unacquainted with God.

God's Will for Mankind

▶Read 1 Timothy 2:3–4; 2 Peter 3:9

From these verses, what can you conclude about God's will and who He wants to save?

"Whoever wishes, let him take the free gift of the water of life" (Revelation 22:17). You heard this invitation and responded. It is God's will that others should hear it—through you. Let it happen!

Week Twelve: The Church in Action—II

Day Two: A Heart of Love

Key Verses: Deuteronomy 10:19; Matthew 22:39; Romans 12:9; 1 Thessalonians 3:12

We have seen that the command to spread the gospel was given by Jesus Christ before His return to heaven. But elsewhere in the Scriptures we have seen that we are to share the message of salvation not only because Jesus commanded us to, but because we have been given a heart of love for mankind. The command has been given and we ought willingly to serve our Lord and be obedient—out of a heart of gratitude and love.

Love for All

▶Read Deuteronomy 10:19; Matthew 22:39

The Greek word translated "love" in this verse from Matthew is not connected to a hazy, feeling-based definition of that word but to the idea of commitment and devotion that can be a matter of decision, or the will. This is in keeping with the Old Testament (Hebrew) command of Deuteronomy, which was as unusual to the world then as it is now. The trait of humans is to seek their own kind; the trait of God is to seek all peoples. To be godlike, we ought to share the gospel with all people because we love them. Regardless of their personality or their status, we are to love them with Christ's love. When we were in our sins, we too were among the unlovely. But Christ loved us.

His Love Extended

▶Read 1 Thessalonians 3:12

According to this verse, how far should our love extend and who enables us to extend that love?

_____

Sincere Love

▶Read Romans 12:9

Write the first sentence of this verse.

_____

Our love for the world must come from a sincere heart. Insincerity is easily seen by the world, but those who love from sincerity cannot be faulted.

Can you think of some of your friends who need Jesus? Make a list of them and then pray that God will direct you with His love so that He can use you to reach them with the gospel.

_____

_____

_____

Week Twelve: The Church in Action—II

Day Three: Sharing the Faith

Key Verses: Deuteronomy 6:6–7; Psalm 145:4; Matthew 19:13–14; Luke 21:12–15; 2 Timothy 1:5

Now that we understand Jesus' command and the kind of attitude out of which we're supposed to share, consider the opportunities you may have for such sharing of your faith.

Within the Family

▶Read Deuteronomy 6:6–7

This instruction was for parents. Parents are to teach their children about God and His Word. Notice the setting for this instruction. Is it formal or informal?

If your family is not Christian, watch for natural opportunities to witness. But be especially sensitive in this approach. They will not likely respond positively to being "preached at." (Consider 1 Peter 3:1–2.)

One Generation to Another

▶Read Psalm 145:4; 2 Timothy 1:5

Preschoolers want to imitate first graders; elementary children stand in awe of young teens; high schoolers are impressed with collegians: The older generation influences the younger. Take advantage of that by influencing for Christ those who look up to you.

Don't Overlook Children

▶Read Matthew 19:13–14

Don't overlook opportunities to bring the good news of the gospel to children. If you enjoy being around children, follow that inclination, perhaps by being part of a backyard Bible club or a vacation Bible school. Children's experiences with adults can stay with them a lifetime. Make a good impression for God in young lives.

Before Authorities

▶Read Luke 21:12–15

Jesus warned the disciples about the opposition they could expect in their generation. You could face something similar, that is, be called before authorities because of your Christian witness. Why do you not need to worry about appearing before such authorities? (See also 1 Peter 3:13–17.)

Pray today that God will help you see any opportunity for sharing His love. Always make your prayer, "Use me, Lord!"

Week Twelve: The Church in Action—II

Day Four: Discipling—The Next Step

Key Verses: Matthew 28:19; John 8:31; Acts 18:26; 1 Corinthians 10:31 to 11:1; 1 Peter 2:21

The church must fully understand the commission the Lord has given. God is not finished with a person after he accepts Jesus as Savior any more than He was finished with you after you accepted Him. As was noted last week, God's work of grace continues through teaching, discipling.

Christ's Command

▶Read Matthew 28:19

This is a challenge we have seen before. Notice that the call is to "make disciples" of all nations. To make disciples means to help others become like Jesus. That involves training in spiritual growth, much like this course seeks to develop in your life.

Obedience

▶Read John 8:31; 1 Peter 2:21

What message do these two verses teach us?

Being obedient to Christ's teaching is what discipleship is all about. Jesus said, "If you hold to my teaching, you are really my disciples."

Discipleship is instruction in and obedience to the commands of Christ. If Christians do not know what the Lord has called them to be or how He wants them to act, then they will be unsuccessful in their efforts to be like Him.

Example

▶Read 1 Corinthians 10:31 to 11:1

You may not realize it but you are already involved in discipling—as an example. But you can go beyond that by contributing to the lives of believers in direct ways: participating in the worship service, welcoming the newcomer, helping where you can, encouraging whoever needs it. (Consider the following verses: Ecclesiastes 4:9–10; John 13:35; 1 Corinthians 14:26; Galatians 6:2; Ephesians 4:29; 1 Thessalonians 5:11.)

Instruction

▶Read Acts 18:26

Apollos was a young man who had an intense desire to share the gospel. But he needed more teaching. God used Aquila and Priscilla, two spiritually mature believers, to help him.

God will use people to guide you, and He wants to use you to guide others. We never come to the place where we need no further teaching from God for our lives. May the Lord help us to always see both our need for instruction and our need to instruct others—by word *and* deed.

Week Twelve: The Church in Action—II

Day Five: Reaching the World

Key Verses: Exodus 17:11–13; 2 Kings 4:8–10; Mark 6:7–10; Luke 8:1–3; Romans 15:23–24; 16:1–2

Throughout this final study, we will focus our attention on the cooperative effort the church makes to get the good news out to all people everywhere: our attempt in this age to carry the gospel "to the ends of the earth" (Acts 1:8).

Old Testament Examples

▶Read Exodus 17:11–13; 2 Kings 4:8–10

Helping one another should be a characteristic of God's people, especially when the extension of God's kingdom is involved. In these two episodes, which one might represent the material support we can provide and which one the spiritual support?

___

___

Jesus' Example

▶Read Luke 8:1–3

Jesus accepted people to meet the human needs He and His disciples had as they went about ministering. What does this say to you?

___

Jesus' Instruction

▶Read Mark 6:7–10

Jesus sent His disciples out "two by two", that is, they went out in partnership (see Ecclesiastes 4:9–12). He taught them to pray together (Matthew 18:19). He taught them also to depend on the hospitality of those they ministered to (Mark 6:7–10). For those being sent as well as for those receiving them, Jesus taught a cooperative effort in ministry.

Paul's Instruction and Example

▶Read Romans 15:23–24; 16:1–2

It is true that Paul was a tentmaker and could support himself (Acts 18:3). And he was careful not to encourage laziness, going so far as to forego what he believed he was entitled to (2 Thessalonians 3:6–10). Nevertheless, he believed, with Jesus, that "those who preach the gospel should receive their living from the gospel" (1 Corinthians 9:14; Luke 10:5–7).

So besides developing the life-style of a witness, support—materially and spiritually—those whose calling to spread the gospel makes them dependent on it for their livelihood. And finally, consider such a vocation for yourself. It may be God's calling for you.

Week Twelve: The Church in Action—II

Day Six

Verses of the Bible I read:

What did they teach me?

What questions do I have?

What do I need to talk to God about?

Week Twelve: The Church in Action—II

Day Seven

What has God shown me through His Word this week?

What questions do I have?

What changes have I seen in my life this week?

How would I explain what Jesus Christ has done for me?